Rawls, Citizenship, and Education

Routledge Studies in Contemporary Philosophy

Rawls, Citizenship, and Education

M. Victoria Costa

Routledge
Taylor & Francis Group

NEW YORK AND LONDON

First published 2011
by Routledge
270 Madison Avenue, New York, NY 10016

Simultaneously published in the UK
by Routledge
2 Park Square, Milton Park, Abingdon, Oxon OX14 4RN

Routledge is an imprint of the Taylor & Francis Group, an informa business

© 2011 Taylor & Francis

Typeset in Sabon by Taylor & Francis Books
Printed and bound in the United States of America on acid-free paper by IBT Global

Library of Congress Cataloging in Publication Data
Costa, M. Victoria.
Rawls, citizenship, and education / by M. Victoria Costa.
p. cm.—(Routledge studies in contemporary philosophy; 21)
Includes bibliographical references (p.) and index.
ISBN 978-0-415-87795-4
1. Citizenship. 2. Citizenship—Study and teaching. 3. Democracy and education. 4. Rawls, John, 1921-2002. I. Title.
JF801.C665 2010
323.6—dc22
2010004026

ISBN13: 978-0-415-87795-4 (hbk)
ISBN13: 978-0-203-84662-9 (ebk)

For Joshua

Contents

Acknowledgments

I began work on this book in 2007, when I received a post-doctoral fellowship from the National Academy of Education and the Spencer Foundation. This fellowship allowed me to devote the 2007–8 academic year to work full time on this project. I have also received funding from a research grant by the Argentine Agency For Scientific Advancement. My co-director in this grant was María Julia Bertomeu.

Although I have benefited from many discussions on parts of this book I would especially like to thank those who gave me written comments on specific chapters: María Julia Bertomeu, Elizabeth Brake, Harry Brighouse, Eamonn Callan, Joshua Gert, Colin Macleod, David McNaughton, and three anonymous reviewers from Routledge. I am especially grateful to María Julia, Eamonn, and Josh, with whom I have had countless philosophical discussions, without which the book would have been very different.

A shorter version of chapter 4 was presented at the 2009 American Philosophical Association Eastern Division Meeting, in a session of the Association for Philosophy of Education. This session was organized by Harry Brighouse and chaired by Randall Curren. My respondents were Elizabeth Brake and Colin Macleod. I am very grateful to all of them for a very enjoyable and useful discussion.

A very short version of chapter 7 was presented at the Annual Meeting of the National Academy of Education, held at the University of Washington in October 2008.

Part of chapter 8 was presented at Teachers College, Columbia University in October 2009. Thanks to David Hansen for inviting me to give this paper, and for causing me to rethink my views on cosmopolitanism.

Three of the chapters contain material previously published in the form of articles. Chapter 5 is based on "Rawlsian Civic Education: Political, not Minimal," *Journal of Applied Philosophy* 21, 1, 2004, 1–14. Chapter 6 is a slight expansion of the paper "Rawls on Liberty and Domination," *Res Publica* 15, 4, 2009, 397–413, printed with kind permission from Springer Science + Business Media. Chapter 7 was published as "Justice as Fairness, Civic Identity and Patriotic Education," *Public Affairs Quarterly* 23, 2, 2009,

95–114. I thank the editors of these journals for permission to reproduce these articles here.

I would also like to thank my friends and family in Argentina and in the United States for their support and encouragement over the years I have been working on this book. This includes those who love philosophy as much as I do (there are four other professional philosophers in my family) and those who do not understand how I can spend so much time reading philosophy, but who persist in encouraging me anyway.

1 Introduction

From the earliest writings on political philosophy to the present day, philosophers have been theorizing about citizenship and the type of education that best encourages its development. The works of Plato, Aristotle, John Locke, Jean Jacques Rousseau, Mary Wollstonecraft, John Stuart Mill, and John Dewey are among the most well-known in this regard. Although not all of these philosophers provided fully developed accounts of the kind of education favored by their political theories, they all recognized the need to educate the younger members of society, whether for the purpose of reproducing the social order or for the purpose of radically transforming it.[1] Contemporary political philosophy is no exception to this historical pattern. The last few decades have witnessed a revival of interest in the topic of citizenship, and in the particular contribution that different types of educational institutions such as families and schools can make to secure the enjoyment of rights and the fulfillment of responsibilities by members of future generations.[2]

Recent philosophical debates on citizenship and education are distinctive in that they reflect a number of concerns related to the political, cultural, and social conditions of the contemporary world.[3] For example, one shared premise in these debates—a premise that has by no means been uniformly endorsed by philosophers in the past—is that all members of democratic societies should be considered as free and equal and that, as a consequence, educational institutions should be designed to uphold their freedom and equality of status. But agreement on this general premise does not always translate into consensus on policy, even among those truly interested in promoting justice (instead of mere factional interests). This is partly because there are a host of alternative ways of conceptualizing freedom and equality, and also because there are disputes regarding which institutional arrangements would best secure the status of citizens as free and equal. Accordingly, some disputes over the ways in which educational institutions should be set up can be traced to disagreements regarding the correct interpretation of the normative political ideals of freedom and equality—or of other competing political ideals such as virtue, utility, or legitimacy—and their implications. But other disputes have empirical sources having to do with the foreseeable consequences of alternative policies in particular social contexts. Empirical research may help resolve some of these disagreements by providing information about, for example, the kind of educational environments that are most favorable for children's academic success, or for their developing civic virtues such as tolerance and mutual respect. But empirical research cannot replace the task of normative assessment of policy, which depends on a thorough consideration of the reasons that justify selecting one particular policy from the wide range of possibilities. A significant amount of empirical research is in fact guided by a set of (more or less implicit) normative ideals. For instance, interest in the study of differences in the educational achievements of children of different gender, ethnicity, or socioeconomic background is in part motivated by the assumption that some children may be suffering as a result of prejudice or unfair social disadvantages which affect their performance in school and their future prospects in life. Empirical research that addresses this type of phenomena is considered useful because acquiring deeper knowledge in the area may help us to design policies that are aimed at combating prejudice and correcting or compensating for unfairness. But our understanding of situations as unfair of course presupposes some notion of what a fair and truly supportive educational and social environment for children and young people would look like. As we pursue a better understanding of our social world, it is as important to clarify and refine these and similar normative assumptions as it is to gather more empirical information about the complex causal relationships that hold between social phenomena.

However, despite an appropriate concern with normative issues, contemporary literature on citizenship and education tends to pay a disproportionate amount of attention to a relatively small subset of these issues: those that are the source of public controversies. For example, a surprisingly large number of articles and book chapters have been written on certain specific judicial decisions regarding exceptions to state educational requirements for Amish or Christian Fundamentalist children in the United States. Similarly, there is a very substantial literature about the political disputes surrounding Muslim girls' use of headscarves in public schools in France.[4] Academic fascination with these types of cases may be due to the fact that they serve to test the limits of the educational authority of liberal democratic states when these come up against the demands of religious citizens. Other controversial topics that are receiving increasing attention are also related to educational policy and religion. Two examples are the permissibility of state funding of religious schools via educational vouchers or other policies and the permissibility of religious practices in public schools.[5] But there are many other important and perhaps more basic normative questions concerning educational policy in liberal democratic societies that are worth examining, even though they do not tend to make the headlines or end up in court.

The questions that I am interested in examining in this book concern the role that public and private educational institutions play—or should play—in the construction of more just and more democratic societies: societies that offer adequate enjoyment of liberties, opportunities, and resources to all their members. In seeking to answer these kinds of questions we can learn from political philosophers of the past who explicitly considered the problem of determining the proper way to educate citizens. In discussing this problem, philosophers were guided by political theories containing well-developed pictures of the types of society and government they regarded as most desirable. It is true that many of their views about desirable social and political arrangements are deeply mistaken and unacceptable in light of our contemporary commitment to democracy as the only legitimate form of government and to the moral equality of all human beings. But my point is that an examination of proposals for educating citizens is more fruitful when aided by a clear account of the type of society and government that underlie such proposals. Accordingly, it is the goal of this book to provide a systematic exploration of the role of education for the promotion of social justice that is based on a well-developed and widely endorsed account of social justice: John Rawls' theory of justice.

Rawls' work on social justice has had an enormous impact in the development of political philosophy over the last four decades.[6] His first book, *A Theory of Justice*, was published in 1971. This was a time in which practical philosophy was dominated by the study of moral and political language and reasoning—in particular, by the study of their formal or logical features. There was widespread skepticism about the possibility of developing moral and political theories with substantive normative implications. Instead of offering theories designed to systematize and explain our judgments about what is right and wrong, or just and unjust, philosophers were discussing the meanings of normative terms and the logical relations among propositions that contained them. Rawls' work was a sharp departure from this metaethical focus and marked a return to systematic normative theorizing. Not only did his work offer novel philosophical arguments for the justification of normative claims, but it also provided a new way of thinking about the justice of a society's main institutions, laws, and policies by developing a set of substantive principles of justice that could be used to assess the joint functioning of those institutions, laws, and policies. Subsequent writing in political philosophy has been significantly shaped by Rawls' theory and by his general approach, even in the work of critics who think his views are deeply misguided and who want to propose alternatives.

Without having "changed the field" in a similar way, Rawls' theory of justice as fairness has already been applied to the discussion of a number of topics in the philosophy of education.[7] However, most of the philosophical work on education that qualifies (in broad terms) as Rawlsian is not really intended to be taken as a systematic exploration of the educational implications of Rawls' theory. Rather, their authors make use of selective elements of Rawls—such as his views on reasonability, the political justification for the use of state power, or the idea of an overlapping consensus—to argue for their own conclusions about the type of education that is most appropriate for future citizens of liberal democracies. As a consequence of this selective use of Rawls' theory, it is sometimes difficult to get a clear view of the extent to which the core prescriptions of the theory of justice as fairness are endorsed by authors who employ a broadly Rawlsian framework or terminology.[8] Given that many readers concerned with educational policy may not be familiar with Rawls' vast work, this book begins with an overview of his method for conceptualizing the philosophical problem of social justice. Once we have a picture of what a just society looks like according to justice as fairness, then we will be in a better position to discuss the kind of education that children should receive, both at home and in schools, if they are to develop their sense of justice and their capacities to live good lives. We will also be in a better position to discuss what schools can do to promote social justice, within the limits of their legitimate educational authority. Rawls' theory implies that children should have guaranteed access to primary and secondary education of high quality roughly until they are 18 years old, and that they should also have fair opportunity to access higher education. Although these claims have independent plausibility, they receive additional support from the fact that they are consequences of a general theory of justice that readers might find attractive and plausible as well. My presentation aims to show that justice as fairness can be used as a basis for developing, clarifying, and evaluating policy, and that the plausibility of its implications lends support to the theory as a coherent articulation of democratic values.

In the first part of the book (chapters 2 and 3) I offer a presentation of the central aspects of John Rawls' theory of justice as fairness. This presentation combines important elements of Rawls' first book, *A Theory of Justice*, with newer elements introduced in *Political Liberalism*, in *Justice as Fairness: A Restatement*, as well as in a number of other works.[9] It is not my aim to examine in detail the evolution of Rawls' thought on social justice. Nor am I interested in stressing the tensions between his earlier and later work. Rather, I will provide a reconstruction of the core normative and methodological commitments of the definitive version of his theory, and then go on to discuss the contribution that educational institutions can and should make for the achievement of social justice according to such a theory. My presentation will distinguish what Rawls said about social justice and policy from what I take to follow from what he said. In this way readers can make up their own minds regarding the plausibility of my interpretation. In my view, the educational literature that relies on Rawls' work has tended to overlook important lessons of *A Theory of Justice* and has placed a disproportionate emphasis on the notions of legitimacy and political justification, which are the more explicit focus of his later works. Although Rawls did not discuss educational policy in detail, and some of his remarks suggest a quite minimalist account of the aims of education, I will argue that the definitive version of justice as fairness supports a robust and progressive account of the role of education in a liberal democratic society. In other words, educational institutions have a significant role to play in the promotion of social justice while respecting pluralism and social diversity.

With a systematic interpretation of Rawls to work from, chapter 4 is devoted to a discussion of the family, which is for Rawls the first educational institution. The status of the family in Rawls' theory of justice is a subject of considerable debate. Many critics of Rawls are puzzled by his claim that the principles of justice do not apply directly to the family. But there is a simple explanation for this claim: for Rawls, the principles apply to the functioning of the set of major social and political institutions taken as a unit. The family is only one part of the whole unit, and cannot be evaluated in isolation. As I will argue, when we assess the family as an educational and distributional institution, we need to keep in mind that its effects are combined with and affected by those of schools, the labor market, and other social and political institutions. Within this network, the family has a significant role to play as the first "school of justice," in which children begin to develop their moral and political capacities.[10] But because not all families provide a perfectly supportive environment for the moral and political development of children, and because families cannot possibly mirror the diversity and complexity of the wider society, their role in the development of reasonable citizens needs to be supplemented by schools. As part of a complex network of institutions, the family also plays a significant distributional role. As regards adult family members, the arrangements of any particular family involve a distribution of paid work and of the task of caring for children and other domestic tasks, and this distribution can be more or less fair. But more importantly for our focus in this book, families also affect children's educational success, since some families are more encouraging than others, or have more resources available with which they can support their children's education. Although Rawls does not discuss these topics in any detail, I will argue that his theory makes room for family partiality. That is, his theory counts it as legitimate for family members to promote their children's education, even though this has an effect on the working of the principle of fair equality of opportunity. But again, this is permissible only provided that the basic structure of society compensates for this effect. And it is schools that are the best candidates to play the compensatory role, so that the set of central social and political institutions satisfy the principles of justice.

Having discussed the educational role of the family on a Rawlsian view, I shift the focus in the remainder of the book to the civic aims of schools. I argue that schools play a key role in reproducing citizens' support for just institutions over time, or in contributing to the creation of just institutions. One of the goals I pursue in chapters 5, 6, 7, and 8 is conceptual: to expand on Rawls' account of citizenship. I examine what it means to say that society should treat its citizens as free and equal, as well as what kinds of dispositions and attitudes, in citizens, support the maintenance of just institutions that treat them in this way. But I also have a practical goal in mind in these chapters: to shed some light on the contribution that schools, both public and private, can make to the cultivation, in citizens, of the complex set of capacities for what Rawls calls "reasonability." Chapter 5 discusses the ways in which the capacities for reasonability can be legitimately cultivated by schools. This task is more difficult than it might seem at first, since Rawls endorses some restrictions on the ways in which policies in pluralistic societies may be justified, and the defense of policies for civic education must therefore take these restrictions into account. In other words: Rawls requires the justification of public policy to be "political." This means that public policy must be justified by appealing to considerations that reasonable people with very different understandings of the good life could accept. My conclusion is that Rawls' overall theory requires more robust forms of civic education than Rawls' own remarks suggest, but that this robust form of civic education counts as "political" in Rawls' sense, because it can be justified appealing to public reasons.

There is a tendency to interpret Rawls' first principle of justice as endorsement of an ideal of freedom as non-interference. But Philip Pettit has recently defended a distinct account of freedom as non-domination that takes the paradigm of a lack of freedom to be a state of slavery or servitude. Chapter 6 extends the robust Rawlsian account by clarifying the ways in which Rawls' theory can be seen to be committed to a political ideal of freedom as non-domination (even though Rawls himself does not use this terminology). If my argument in this chapter is correct, there is a case for an education for freedom as non-domination that is different from the more common defenses of education for autonomy that appear in the literature. I argue that domination is an evil that undermines citizens' status as free and equal, and that education for non-domination can be defended in Rawlsian "political" terms, since a just society cannot condone serious forms of domination. In educational terms, civic education can make an important contribution to prevent state domination, as well as interpersonal relationships of domination and servility.

In chapter 7 I discuss the question of whether or not Rawls' account of reasonable citizens should be extended to include the cultivation of patriotic identifications. Some critics of Rawls claim that schools should encourage patriotism, understood as an identification with a particular people and its political institutions. In support of this idea, they claim that patriotism provides indispensable motivation for citizens to support fair social arrangements of the kind that satisfy Rawls' principles of justice. After considering a variety of instrumental and non-instrumental arguments for the teaching of patriotism, I conclude that teaching patriotism in actual (that is, imperfect) societies has many moral liabilities, and that it is better to focus on the teaching of principles of justice and the ways in which actual institutions (imperfectly) embody them. In chapter 8, I go on to discuss whether Rawls' account of reasonable citizens should be extended in another direction: to include positive attitudes towards social and cultural diversity, and a willingness to find fair ways of accommodating cultural differences in society. In contrast to my answer in the case of patriotic feelings, my answer to this question is positive. But I also expect my answer will be somewhat controversial. In particular, I argue for two conclusions. First, if a society is to work according to the principles of justice, then there must be policies that facilitate the voluntary integration of cultural minorities (immigrants and national minorities) into major social institutions, such as the political system. But, second, justice does not require public support for relatively separate social institutions for cultural minorities. In particular, it discourages certain forms of separate schooling and other educational policies designed to support the cultivation of quasi separatist forms of national identity. I argue in favor of teaching the principles of justice and cultivating attitudes and dispositions that support fair social arrangements, while encouraging a sense of belonging to the political community as a whole.

2   What is a Just Society?

The Subject of Justice

Although there are different sorts of entities that we may properly call just or unjust—people, contracts, punishments, or rules, to give just a few examples—Rawls is clear that the primary subject of his theory of justice is what he calls "the basic structure of society."[1] This basic structure can be thought of as the structure of a complex whole, made up of the set of major social institutions as they function together as a system, distributing rights and duties, as well as other benefits and burdens of social cooperation, among citizens. Rawls suggests that in order to assess whether and to what degree a society is just, one should not look at the workings of particular social institutions in isolation, or at the individual behavior of its citizens. Rather, one should focus on the ways in which the major social institutions interact in one large scheme. It is true that a close examination of one major social institution, such as the legal system, may provide us with significant information as we seek to establish how just a society is overall. But a better way to evaluate the level of justice of a society requires us to look at the operation of all the major social institutions taken together as an integrated whole. One reason to take this more comprehensive view is that a certain level of injustice in one type of major social institution might be mitigated (or aggravated) by the workings of the others.

Not all social institutions count as part of the basic structure for Rawls. As examples of institutions that belong to the basic structure he cites "the political constitution, the legally recognized forms of property, and the organization of the economy, and the nature of the family."[2] These institutions can themselves be understood as public systems of rules: rules that define a set of offices and positions and that assign the rights and duties that attach to each of them.[3] According to Rawls, the institutions that belong to the basic structure have a deep and pervasive effect, not only on the lives and future prospects of all citizens, but also on their characters, aims, and aspirations. These institutions are central to social life and necessary for the continued existence of society. The basic structure shapes the way a society "produces and reproduces over time a certain form of culture shared by persons with certain conceptions of their good."[4] Although Rawls does not mention schools when he offers his list of major social institutions, his characterization of the basic structure suggests that the educational system should also be counted as a part of it. One reason for this is the obvious role schools play in the reproduction of a society's culture among its youngest members. Another reason is that access to different levels of education reliably affect the life prospects of children (for example, their access to desirable jobs and a good income).[5]

There are a number of important points that follow from Rawls' understanding of the basic structure as the primary subject of justice. One is that a focus on the major social institutions allows us to conceptualize justice (or injustice) as structural. That is, it allows us to see more clearly that the origins of injustice cannot be strictly understood in terms of individual behavior. In particular, injustice may sometimes be the result of complex interactions of rules and of aggregated individual behavior regulated by such rules, even in situations in which there is nothing morally objectionable about any of the individual behavior itself.[6] As will become clear after our examination of the two particular principles of justice that Rawls defends, the principles of justice that regulate the basic structure are very different from the moral principles or moral rules that apply directly to the actions of individual citizens in particular circumstances. Although the two sorts of principles are interconnected, Rawls thinks that the normative evaluation of the set of major social institutions (and of institutions in general) should be kept distinct from the normative evaluation of individual behavior. But the fact that the principles that apply to institutions are different from those that apply to individual people by no means implies that just institutions can be maintained over time independently of the beliefs, attitudes, and behavior of citizens. This is one reason why the education of citizens is so central to the quest to achieve and sustain a just society. Nor does the distinction between the two sorts of principles imply that individual behavior and its proper moral assessment are independent of institutional functioning. Because institutional schemes regulate and facilitate interactions between individuals, they must be taken into account when assessing the morality of individual actions. Jon Mandle nicely highlights the many ways in which institutional contexts and institutional roles have an impact on individual behavior:

> As participants in economic institutions, we make decisions regarding our employers, employees, and co-workers; as family members, we make decisions regarding our parents, children, siblings, and loved ones; as participants in our political institutions, we consider how to vote, whom to lobby, and whether to demonstrate.[7]

Mandle argues that in order to provide an adequate account of the morality of individual actions, and of the moral character of people, we have to acknowledge the centrality of institutional contexts. This is because a significant portion of our moral obligations are based on institutional roles.

A further point regarding Rawls' focus on the basic structure is that he takes this focus to be equivalent to adopting a society or country as the preferred level at which his theory applies.[8] Of course Rawls does not deny the importance of local justice (that is, the justice of particular local institutions or associations), or of global justice.[9] But his theory of justice as fairness is set up to justify principles of justice that are appropriately applied *only* to the basic structure of a democratic society, and this is important because such principles may not be easily transferable to other levels.[10] This implication about the scope of the theory has become more explicit in Rawls' later work on international justice, in which the principles he proposes to regulate international relations are quite different from the principles for the domestic level.[11] This difference can be explained, in general terms, by the fact that the principles apply to different kinds of institutions. As Andrea Sangiovanni has made clear, on an approach such as Rawls', the content and justification of the principles of justice depend on the particular kind of institutional structure they are meant to regulate.[12] This approach to the justification of principles of justice assumes that the nature of the shared social and political institutions affects the relationships between people in a way that is relevant to the kind of principles that are appropriate for them.

Not only does Rawls' theory of justice as fairness focus exclusively on the level of a country, it is restricted in another way as well: it is meant to regulate the working of institutions that mediate the relations among citizens of a *democratic* society. For this reason, the construction of the theory of justice as fairness begins by taking into account certain facts about democratic societies and by providing an interpretation of the function of the major social and political institutions in such societies.[13] One of these facts is that of pluralism, that is, the fact that citizens do not all agree on the ultimate values that define the good life. There are, therefore, a plurality of views regarding what is valuable to pursue in life, including views about which personal virtues and interpersonal relationships are worth cultivating. But the existence, in democratic societies, of a plurality of moral, religious, and philosophical doctrines about the good should not be understood as the result of the failure of some citizens to exercise reason properly. Rather, Rawls claims that we must see such disagreements as the inevitable outcome of life under free institutions. Indeed, he provides some explanation—which we will examine in chapter 3—for the fact that even citizens whose reasoning involves neither error nor ignorance may nevertheless come to different conclusions on certain central issues. One important consequence of all this is the following: because citizens have common and conflicting interests, as well as different views about the good, the major social institutions in democratic societies should be set up in such a way that they mediate fairly among them.

The Political Justification of Justice as Fairness

Rawls argues that a theory of justice that is appropriate for democratic societies—societies in which, among other things, there is a plurality of views of the good life—has to satisfy certain requirements if it is to count as providing a "political justification" for its principles. This is important because unless it can provide a political justification for its principles it will be incapable of gaining the reasoned support of citizens who have very different ways of understanding the good life. According the Rawls, a theory counts as a political theory when it satisfies three requirements concerning its subject, status, and source of justification.[14] The first requirement on a political theory of justice is that it have a restricted subject: the basic structure of society. As we have seen, this means that the theory applies to the interrelated workings of the major political, social, and economic institutions of society. Such a theory will not pretend to have a more general scope. It will not provide answers to questions about what justice requires in every situation; nor will it provide principles for the regulation of every sort of institution or association, or of detailed aspects of the personal lives of citizens. Second, a political theory of justice should be presented as freestanding, that is, it does not derive from any particular comprehensive doctrine about the good. This means that the central notions involved in the theory do not depend on philosophical, religious, or moral views about how people should live their lives in general. Rather, the theory is justified in such a way that it can be acceptable to citizens who adhere to a variety of different comprehensive views about the good. Third, the content of the theory should be developed on the basis of certain fundamental ideas that are seen as implicit in the public culture of a democratic society. The public culture includes the political institutions of a constitutional regime, as well as the public tradition of their interpretation. In this way, the theory attempts to offer a systematic articulation of certain intuitive ideas embodied in the main political and social institutions, ideas that can be seen as implicitly shared.

The core normative commitments of Rawls' theory of justice are contained in two principles of justice which will be examined in the next section. Rawls uses two intuitive ideas—taken from the public culture—to develop his main arguments for the two principles of justice (a) that society should be understood, ideally, as a fair system of cooperation and (b) that citizens are free and equal.[15] Let us briefly examine these two ideas. As Rawls understands it, the idea of society as a fair system of cooperation presupposes that there are publicly recognized rules and procedures that regulate social life, and that these rules and procedures are such that all citizens may reasonably accept them. The terms of social cooperation are fair, according to Rawls, when they express an idea of reciprocity: everyone does her part voluntarily as required by the rules and procedures, and everyone benefits from the resulting joint social activity. To clarify the intuitions behind this idea, we can contrast a situation of reciprocity with a situation in which some people are forced into servitude, so that their work is not voluntarily undertaken and does not benefit them. The idea of society as a system of cooperation requires that the shared activity of society must, from each participant's point of view, be to her rational advantage or good.[16] This idea of society makes room for citizens pursuing their conceptions of the good, but also requires their joint commitment to sustain just background institutions.

In order for just social arrangements among the citizens of a society to be possible, there are certain characteristics that these citizens themselves must possess. As part of an explanation of these characteristics, Rawls offers a particular interpretation of the general idea that citizens are free and equal.[17] His interpretation of this idea involves their possessing two particular moral capacities, as well as rational capacities in general. The first of the moral capacities is the capacity for a sense of justice: the ability to understand, apply, and act according to just rules and procedures. The second moral capacity is the capacity for a conception of the good: the ability to form, and revise, a scheme of ends or goals that one wants to realize in one's life. This scheme of ends includes attachments and loyalties to individuals and groups, because for (almost) all of us, the good of others who are close to us is part of our conception of the good. Citizens' conceptions of the good are sometimes integrated into more general religious, philosophical, or moral comprehensive doctrines that explain the value and significance of such ends and attachments, but they need not be. Now, Rawls claims that citizens are considered free because, for political purposes, they are not seen as inevitably tied to or determined by the conception of the good they happen to hold true. But he also maintains that citizens are considered free in a second sense: we think of citizens as the sources of valid claims, that is, we think that citizens are entitled to certain rights. And, finally, citizens are considered free because we regard them as responsible for the ends they take up. So the freedom of citizens, for Rawls, involves the following three aspects: freedom from any particular conception of the good, freedom associated with rights, and freedom associated with responsibility. Rawls' explanation of the relevant sense of equality at work in the ideal of citizens as free and equal is simpler. It involves only the fact that citizens are equal by virtue of having the two moral capacities and other rational capacities to a minimum requisite degree, so that they can be fully cooperating members of society.[18]

Arguments for the Principles of Justice

On the basis of these two ideas present in the public culture—of society as a fair system of cooperation and of citizens as free and equal—Rawls develops his argument for the principles of justice, introducing a thought-experiment that has at its center a device known as the "original position." The original position is a hypothetical situation that somehow corresponds to the idea of society as a fair system of cooperation among free and equal citizens. In particular, it describes a set of fair conditions under which the representatives of citizens come to an agreement about the basic terms of social cooperation. The original position is meant to play a central role in a systematic argument for the justification of principles of justice. Once we have a set of principles that would be chosen in a certain version of the original position, the principles themselves can be independently assessed taking into account their intuitive plausibility. This assessment may itself lead to some changes in the way the original position is conceived. The thought-experiment can then be repeated, yielding slightly different principles, which are then assessed. And the process repeats until we reach a stable equilibrium.

The original position involves representatives of citizens—sometimes also called 'parties'—and Rawls proposes that we imagine these representatives or parties as if they were located behind a "veil of ignorance." This means that the representatives do not know the social position of those they represent, or the comprehensive doctrine about the good that they endorse. Nor do they have information about their race, ethnicity, sex, natural capacities, talents, or other personal characteristics. But the parties are not completely ignorant. They have knowledge of certain facts about social organization, political affairs, economics, and human psychology, and this knowledge helps them decide which principles are more plausibly regarded as leading to stable social cooperation.[19]

The restrictions on the information available to the representatives who will select the principles of justice are designed to remove the possibility of negotiating unfair advantages, and this is meant to ensure that the selected principles will be acceptable to all and will respect everyone's claims to be treated as free and equal. In *A Theory of Justice*, Rawls justified the selection of the principles in the original position by making certain claims about what is rational to choose under the specified conditions of uncertainty, together with other assumptions about the motivation and psychology of the parties. But later Rawls came to see these claims about rationality as too controversial to provide the basis for a political justification of the principles – in the sense of 'political' explained earlier. His later view, as represented in *Political Liberalism*, is that the balance of reasons favors the selection of his two principles of justice as the most appropriate for the development and exercise of citizens' central moral capacities. That is, his principles best allow citizens to develop the capacities to propose, and comply with, fair terms of cooperation, as well as to form, pursue, and revise their own conceptions of the good. Although he does not provide an extensive new political argument for the selection of his particular principles of justice, he offers a number of brief discussions that allow us to reconstruct some of the reasons that he thinks tip the balance in favor of these principles, as against other alternatives. Here are a few of the most important of these considerations.

If the principles of justice are to specify fair terms of cooperation among citizens with different conceptions of the good, we need some common currency in terms of which we can discuss what is to their rational advantage or promotes their good. For this purpose, Rawls proposes a "thin" account of the good that appeals to a relatively short list of primary social goods. This list of primary goods allows us to make interpersonal comparisons among citizens with very different conceptions of the good life. By looking at the quantities of primary goods that different people have, we can distinguish between those who are in more and less advantaged positions. A list of the primary social goods is as follows:

(a) First, the basic liberties as given by a [second] list, for example: freedom of thought and liberty of conscience; freedom of association; the freedom defined by the liberty and integrity of the person, as well as by the rule of law; and finally the political liberties;
(b) Second, freedom of movement and choice of occupation against a background of diverse opportunities;
(c) Third, powers and prerogatives of offices and positions of responsibility, particularly those in the main political and economic institutions;
(d) Fourth, income and wealth; and
(e) Finally, the social bases of self-respect.[20]

Rawls is open to the idea that this list of primary goods may need revision, and perhaps some other goods could be added, but for our purposes here we can take the list as definitive.[21] In his earlier work, Rawls describes the primary social goods as all-purpose means: means that it is rational for people to want, regardless of which conception of the good they endorse. Later, he prefers to describe them as goods that are necessary for the development and exercise of the moral capacities of citizens. But these two descriptions of the primary goods are perfectly compatible. The main difference between them is that, according to the latter, basic liberties will be more significant than other goods because they are necessary for the development and exercise of moral capacities. The former description makes the value of the basic liberties, like the value of the other goods, more dependent on the particular conception of the good that a citizen happens to endorse, and people may value some of these goods more than others. For example, some may have an ascetic view of the good life and think that income and wealth are not very valuable. Others may endorse the traditional way of life of the small community in which they grew up, and may not find that having a wide range of opportunities or having freedom of movement is particularly significant for their plan of life. And still others may not be interested in having freedom to express their political, moral, or religious views, and so on. But the point still holds that a citizen of any of these kinds will need a certain minimal package of resources, opportunities, and freedoms if she is to be able to develop and pursue her plan of life, and perhaps, at some point, to revise it.

In the conditions stipulated to hold in the original position, where representatives are deprived of information about the actual conceptions of the good endorsed by the people they represent, there is a presumption in favor of trying to secure as many primary goods as possible. These same restrictions on information are also necessary to guarantee a certain important form of impartiality in negotiations, so that the interests of a variety of people with very different plans of life, different capacities, and different social backgrounds, are all taken into account. Because they result in this form of impartiality, the restrictions on information seem a plausible way to generate fair decisions. Consider what might happen if the representatives were not so restricted. If some of them knew that in the society in which the principles were going to apply there would be a significant majority of Catholics, and that the citizens they represented were Catholic, they might not be willing to accept a principle that guaranteed greater religious freedom or the separation of church and state, and they might argue instead for a policy of highly preferential treatment of the religion of the majority. But it is clear that the fact that someone holds a particular moral, religious, or philosophical doctrine about the good is not a good reason to propose principles that will benefit only those who profess the same doctrine, and that ignore the legitimate claims of others. In the same way, the fact that someone occupies a particular social position is not a good enough reason to support principles, or to expect others to accept principles, that will favor only those in her particular social position. After all, we are trying to figure out what the fair terms of social cooperation are like.

Given that they cannot appeal to considerations that derive from the particular conceptions of the good of the people they represent, Rawls proposes that representatives evaluate alternative principles by taking into account the extent to which these principles would secure access to social primary goods: goods that are required to develop and exercise citizens' moral capacities and that are also general-purpose means for the pursuit of different conceptions of the good. Rawls notes that if representatives take into account the fact of pluralism, they will try to insure against the possibility that the person they represent suffers simply because she is a member of a religious minority or because she subscribes to a comprehensive doctrine that happens to be unpopular. These considerations support the selection of a principle that guarantees a number of basic freedoms to all citizens, and there does not seem to be any good reason to prefer an unequal distribution of basic freedoms, given their importance for the exercise and development of the sense of justice and a conception of the good.[22] Accordingly, representatives in the original position will select the following as the first principle of justice:

> Each person has an equal claim to a fully adequate scheme of equal basic rights and liberties, which scheme is compatible with the same

scheme for all; and in this scheme the equal political liberties, and only those liberties, are to be guaranteed their fair value.[23]

So far we have a political argument in favor of the first principle of justice. However, it is not clear how to construct a unified political argument in support of the selection of Rawls' second principle, which is as follows:

> Social and economic inequalities are to satisfy two conditions: first, they are to be attached to positions and offices open to all under conditions of fair equality of opportunity; and second, they are to be to the greatest benefit of the least advantaged members of society.[24]

This two-part principle secures two benefits, but it also establishes a lexical priority between them. Fair equality of opportunity is to be given priority, and then the distribution of economic resources is to be set up in such as way as to work for the greatest benefit of the least advantaged.

Brian Barry has proposed the following consideration in an effort to provide something like a political justification for the selection of the second part of the second principle: it is plausible to think that representatives would be concerned to eliminate the possibility that those they represent be reduced to an unbearable level of poverty that makes it impossible for them to develop their capacities or pursue their plans of life.[25] For this reason, they might select a principle that requires that social institutions be set up in such a way that the life expectations of the least advantaged are above a certain minimum. But Barry's suggestion is not exactly an argument for the particular content of the second part of the second principle. For that content includes not merely that the least advantaged have certain minimum expectations, but in particular that any inequalities work maximally to their benefit. This latter principle is known as the difference principle. In order to yield the difference principle, the representatives would have to try to ensure that the amount of resources each one gets is as high as possible, keeping in mind that they may be the least-favored members of society. In order to get this result, one might claim that representatives would start by agreeing to an equal distribution of all social and economic resources, trying to secure as many resources as possible for each. Next, they would agree to accept unequal distributions provided that the amount distributed to those who get the least is higher than it would have been had everyone received equal amounts. This could happen under the plausible assumption that social and economic inequalities may sometimes have some useful consequences: for example, their possibility may allow for incentives that in turn generate higher productivity in goods and services. The result of a full series of these revised agreements would be that the worst off do as well as possible.

However, even if the aforementioned considerations are correct, they do not fully explain why representatives should also be interested in securing fair equality of opportunity and its priority over the difference principle.

The difficulty in developing a political justification of the whole of the complex second principle stems from the fact that the principle has two lexically-ordered parts, the first of which secures fair equality of opportunity to access to desirable social positions and the second of which allows inequalities in material resources provided they benefit the least advantaged. Rawls claims that the demands of fair equality of opportunity should be given priority over the demands of the difference principle. And this means that, faced with a choice between institutional arrangement A, which devotes considerable resources to increasing opportunities for education and desirable jobs, and institutional arrangement B, which generates more economic benefits for the least advantaged, the second principle requires that we select arrangement A.

So far we have mentioned two arguments that make use of the original position. One is an argument for equal liberty and the other is an argument for the difference principle. Both of these arguments explain the reasoning of representatives who must take into account the possibility that those they represent are disadvantaged in some respect. In the case of the selection of the principle of liberty, representatives will think about minorities who hold conceptions of the good not shared by the rest of society. In the case of the difference principle, they will take into account the interests of the group of people whose life expectations involve fewer primary goods (or economic resources if we use them as proxy for other primary goods). This group will include those born into less advantaged social positions, who are likely to have fewer opportunities to obtain desirable jobs, and with fewer natural talents, who are likely to have lesser potential to develop marketable skills. But neither of these arguments supports the second principle as Rawls conceives it, since Rawls' conception includes a priority of opportunity over resources. The difficulty of constructing a unified argument for both parts of the second principle and their lexical ordering stems from the plausibility of the idea that the principle of fair equality of opportunity will primarily benefit those who are born in the least advantaged social positions *only if* we also assume that they are naturally talented and motivated to take advantage of the opportunities available. The representatives in the original position could certainly think of the following three types of groups as being disadvantaged by the way the basic structure is set up: (1) those with minority comprehensive doctrines, which may be unpopular, (2) those without natural talents, and (3) those born in less-privileged social positions. The possibility of being disadvantaged for any of the aforementioned reasons will prompt the selection of (1) the principle of liberty, (2) the difference principle, and (3) the fair equality of opportunity principle, respectively. But if we are to defend Rawls' lexical ordering of the fair equality of opportunity over the difference principle we still need some argument to show how the interest in having fair equality of opportunity will have more weight behind the veil of ignorance than the interest in increasing the prospects of obtaining more economic resources.[26]

I do not want to deny the relevance of the two principles of justice in determining what a just basic structure would be like. Nor do I want to deny the plausibility of Rawls' lexical ordering. Moreover, I admit that Rawls does explain why equal basic liberty should have priority over the demands of the second principle, at least in relatively wealthy democratic societies in which citizens' basic needs are already satisfied. The reason is that basic liberties are central for the development and exercise of the moral capacities of citizens, so restrictions on basic liberties would not be justified by the prospect of economic gains. But he does not explain why, in the original position, representatives would decide to give priority to a guarantee of fair equality of opportunity, rather than to a requirement that inequalities work for the benefit of the least advantaged. So my conclusion is that the original position does not provide the basis for an argument for generating the principles and their specific priority, which is what Rawls had intended it to do.

However, once we assess the principles outside of the original position and in the context of relatively wealthy societies, then Rawls' ordering of the principles becomes more plausible. That is, when we lift the veil of ignorance there is a lot of intuitive plausibility to the idea that for a society to be just it must take measures to ensure fair equality of opportunity, and that providing citizens with a wide range of opportunities for the pursuit of their plans of life is more significant than having more economic resources available to all, included the least advantaged (always assuming that important material needs are already satisfied). A society with a basic structure regulated only by the liberty principle and the difference principle seems intuitively unjust to most people. Such a society will secure basic liberties to all its members, and its economic inequalities will work for the benefit of everyone, especially the poorest. But even if the material needs of the poorest members are completely satisfied, their opportunities to access to desirable social positions and jobs might be seriously restricted or non-existent. That is, such a society might afford very few opportunities for social mobility. A conclusion to draw from these reflections is that once important material needs are satisfied, it seems more seriously unjust to fail to provide significant opportunities to access desirable jobs and social positions than to fail to increase the amount of economic resources for the least advantaged to the highest level possible. That is, Rawls' lexical ordering seems correct.

Rawls claims that his two principles of justice should be considered valid, since they result from a procedure that appeals to political ideals that are implicit in the public culture of democratic societies. Moreover, they are not presented as strictly *true*, but rather as the most reasonable, and in principle subject to revision. Rawls avoids commitment to any metaphysical view about the nature of normative principles. He thinks that his principles can be seen as an independent "module" that can fit into different comprehensive doctrines, and that explicit endorsement of metaphysical doctrines would unnecessarily limit the acceptability of the principles. It is important to emphasize that his two principles are meant to do more than merely make explicit the normative judgments that are already endorsed by members of democratic societies. Rawls' argument begins by proposing certain notions that seem intuitively acceptable in light of convictions shared by citizens of democratic societies. It then goes on to design the thought-experiment that includes the device of the original position. The idea is that this thought-experiment is a way of organizing the shared convictions and of using them in a defense of his principles, partly by showing that they form part of a coherent set of normative commitments that receive justification from their mutual support.

Some Implications of the Principles of Justice

Once we have the two principles of justice in hand, and a specification of their lexical ordering as well, we can asses their plausibility in light of our considered judgments about what counts as just or unjust social policy. Rawls' theory proposes that a just society is a society, the basic structure of which is regulated by the two principles of justice. By explicitly examining the implications of the two principles we can get a clearer idea of the picture of a just society that Rawls is proposing.

Let us start with the principle of liberty. This principle secures an equal distribution of basic rights and liberties to all citizens. It implies, among other things, that a society that denies certain basic liberties to its members cannot possibly be regarded as just. Nor can it be considered just if it grants some of these rights and liberties only to a restricted subset of (adult) citizens. But in order to get a more substantial view of the implications of this principle we need some account of which rights and liberties count as basic.[27] Rawls provides the following list of basic rights and liberties:[28]

1. Liberty of conscience and freedom of thought: Liberty of conscience includes the freedom to practice any particular religion, or no religion at all. It also includes the freedom to pursue a set of values grounded in philosophical, moral, or metaphysical views. Freedom of thought extends to the expression of belief regarding a wide variety of subjects, including, for example, art, science, and literature.
2. Freedom of association: This is the liberty to associate with whomever one chooses and to form different sorts of groups with the goal of promoting a variety of ends.
3. Equal political liberties: These include the right to vote and to hold office, freedom of political speech, freedom of assembly, freedom to criticize the government, and to form and join political parties.
4. Rights and liberties that protect the integrity and freedom of the person: These include prohibitions against coercion, physical harm, and enslavement, freedom to choose one's occupation, and a right to hold a certain amount of personal property, among other things.

5. Rights and liberties covered by the rule of law: These include things such as freedom from arbitrary arrest and the seizure of one's property, the right to a fair trial, the right against self-incrimination, and other due process rights. Rawls claims that the rule of law is a precondition for the enjoyment of a number of liberties, because it sets the boundaries between what is legally permissible and what is not, and allows citizens to form reasonable expectations about the behavior of others.

Rawls seems to have produced the list of the basic rights and liberties of citizens primarily by examining the historical development of actual democracies over the past few centuries. This would help explain why it is that it contains such a heterogeneous collection of elements. Certainly the list conspicuously includes the kinds of liberties that were singled out as central during the political struggles that led to their constitutional protection in a number of countries. But Rawls also uses a further criterion to refine the set of liberties that count as basic. This criterion derives from his own conception of citizens as free and equal, with interests in developing and exercising their moral capacities (the capacity for a sense of justice and the capacity for a conception of the good), as well as in pursuing their conceptions of the good.[29] Because he holds this account of freedom and equality, certain rights and liberties do not count as basic for him: those that do not seem to him to be essential to the informed and effective exercise of moral capacities: for example, the right to own the means of production or the right to bear arms.

The liberties in Rawls' list are protected by the rules of legal institutions. As he puts it, "the basic liberties are specified by institutional rights and duties that entitle citizens to do various things, if they wish, and forbid others to interfere. The basic liberties are a framework of legally protected paths and opportunities."[30]

The institutional nature of the basic liberties entails that, to a certain extent, the law and the judicial system will define their scope and limits. But calling these liberties basic also means that governments cannot infringe on them without injustice. Nor can citizens transfer them or trade them for other goods.

Rawls' reference to a right to hold personal property may be the source of some misunderstandings so it is worth clarifying what he takes to be involved in this right. Rawls thinks that the right to personal property is necessary for personal independence, and also for developing a sense of self-respect. According to Samuel Freeman, the right to hold personal property is a right to have

> control over one's living space and a right to enjoy it without interference by the State or others. The reason for this right to personal property is that, without control over personal possessions and quiet

enjoyment of one's own living space, many of the basic liberties cannot be enjoyed or exercised.[31]

If this is the proper justifying explanation of this basic right to hold personal property, then it is worth stressing that it does not amount to a right to unlimited accumulation of property, and it is perfectly compatible with high levels of taxation on income. Nor does the right to personal property involve taking sides on the issue of whether productive property should be privately or collectively owned. Finally, including use of personal property among the basic liberties is not equivalent to guaranteeing access to any particular quantity of economic resources for citizens. This access is guaranteed in Rawls' theory, but the guarantee is provided by the second principle of justice.

Rawls distinguishes between liberties themselves and the "worth of liberty," which can be understood as the potentially variable usefulness that particular liberties can have in different citizens' pursuit of their plans of life.[32] To *have* a liberty is simply to have security against certain forms of interference by other individuals or by the state. But the *worth* that a particular kind of liberty will have for a particular citizen depends on her conception of the good and also on the resources that she has, with which she can take advantage of the liberty. Although Rawls holds that the basic liberties themselves must be equally distributed among citizens, he does not think that the worth of these liberties also needs to be equally distributed. Indeed, he argues that, because the worth of particular liberties is contingent on citizens' conceptions of the good, it is neither desirable nor possible to try to equalize the overall worth of liberty. Suppose, for example, that fulfilling my conception of the good life would require that I make a spiritual trip to India, and that I publish full-page advertisements in major newspapers advocating what I take to be the true path to enlightenment. This will of course consume a significant quantity of my resources. Other people, with different conceptions of the good life, are likely to require far fewer resources to take full advantage of their freedom of religion and freedom of expression. But it does not make sense to conclude that I should therefore receive more resources than others because of my particular understanding of what a significant exercise of my basic liberties requires.

However, there is a special group of basic liberties whose worth Rawls claims in later works should be substantially equal: the political liberties.[33] The idea behind this additional requirement is that we should prevent those with more economic resources from being able to control and influence the outcome of political decisions, since this would lead to their interests' having an undue weight in the adoption of laws and policies. If the political liberties of citizens had a highly unequal worth, citizens' political equality would be endangered. For this reason Rawls thinks that there should be measures such as restrictions on the financing of political campaigns, limits on private political advertisement, access to public broadcasting by political groups, and so on, to prevent those citizens who have more economic resources from dominating the rest of the citizenry and shaping the law in ways that favor their particular interests.

Now let us move on to the first part of the second principle of justice. This principle asserts that social and economic inequalities are acceptable, provided there is fair equality of opportunity to access positions, offices, and desirable jobs.[34] Rawls begins his defense of this principle by insisting on the idea that such goods should be allocated by open competition. We can summarize this idea in the slogan of 'careers open to talents.' One obvious implication of this idea is that there should be no legal restrictions—of a certain sort—on access to desirable social positions. In particular, there should be no legal discrimination on the basis of gender, race, religion, or other factors unrelated to one's qualifications to perform the relevant tasks. But the mere existence of open competition is not enough. Rawls argues that, because educational and job opportunities tend to be greater for those born in privileged social positions, the principle of fair equality of opportunity cannot be satisfied merely by implementing measures to prevent discrimination. Other measures are necessary to correct or at least mitigate social disadvantages. Rawls therefore proposes the following interpretation of the requirement of fair equality of opportunity:

> Offhand it is not clear what is meant, but we might say that those with similar abilities and skills should have similar life chances. More specifically, assuming there is a distribution of natural assets, those who are at the same level of talent and ability, and have the same willingness to use them, should have the same prospects of success regardless of their initial place in the social system. In all sectors of society there should be roughly equal prospects of culture and achievement for everyone similarly motivated and endowed.[35]

According to this principle, steps should be taken to offer educational opportunities that will ensure that people with similar talents and motivations can compete on fair terms for desirable social positions. Andrew Mason correctly points out that the principle of fair equality of opportunity regulates only the workings of the institutions of the basic structure, and is not meant to apply narrowly to individual selection procedures.[36] Thus, the principle looks at the whole set of selection procedures that are made across a society. One interesting consequence of this point is that we cannot properly say that a selection procedure satisfies (or fails to satisfy) the requirements of the principle unless it is part of a set of institutions that guarantees (or fails to guarantee) that those with similar abilities and motivation will have similar life prospects.[37]

Rawls himself acknowledges that there will be many practical difficulties in implementing the principle of fair equality of opportunity, and that it probably can never be completely satisfied.[38] A significant portion of children's early education is provided by their families, and unless we think that families should be abolished, this fact will significantly affect children's future prospects. This suggests that schools should have a significant role in mitigating the inequalities that result from the different types of early non-formal education that children receive. Rawls does not say much about this issue, and he does not take sides on the question of how the school system should be structured. But it is at least quite clear that public regulation is necessary if the principle of equal opportunity is to be satisfied. Letting market forces determine the kinds of educational opportunities available to children, especially those born into the least advantaged social positions, will never lead to similar life chances. However, because education is a complex social good, its value cannot be understood purely instrumentally, as a means to compete successfully for desirable jobs and positions of authority. Rather, education is also necessary for the development of citizens' intellectual and moral capacities, including their sense of justice and their capacity to form a personal plan of life. Thus, there are additional relevant considerations to help us determine how education should be distributed: considerations unrelated to the goal of securing fair equality of opportunity (in the strict sense defined earlier). Some of these additional considerations will lend support to a generous public funding of schools, so that all children and teenagers can achieve a high level of competence.

Most scholarly discussion of Rawls' principles of justice has focused on the second part of the second principle, that is, on the difference principle. Despite what one might initially think, this should not strike us as especially surprising, since this principle is more novel than the other two and also more controversial. This is not the place to review the enormous literature on the difference principle. Rather, I will only briefly present some central points about it, in order to clarify its implications so that we will have a more complete picture of what a just society would be like, according to Rawls' theory. The first thing to notice about this principle is that—as is also true of the first principle and the first part of the second principle—it is not intended to regulate individual behavior or the functioning of particular institutions. Rather, the difference principle applies to an interconnected set of background economic rules, such as the structure of the market, the system of property, taxes, contracts, and other aspects of the economy. The principle says that among alternative ways of structuring the economic system, one should prefer the one that maximally improves the life prospects of those in the least advantaged group, understanding such prospects in terms of social primary goods such as income and wealth. It is important here to note that the least advantaged group must be understood as a certain class: the class of those who are employed and earn the least. A common mistake in discussions of the difference principle consists in thinking that the principle requires maximizing the income of actual individuals who are currently earning the least amount. This leads to the following objection:

the principle would benefit individuals who prefer to work less than others, or who prefer not to work at all, since these people will be the poorest. But Rawls phrases the principle in terms of the lifetime expectations of *representative* individuals. The groups, in reference to which these individuals are taken to be representative, can be described in terms of the natural talents of their members and the social positions into which they are born. Thus, the difference principle says that the set of background rules that regulate the economy should be set up in such a way that the lifetime expectations of those who are born in the least advantaged positions and with the least marketable talents should be increased as much as possible. It is irrelevant— at least to the prospects of formulating an objection to the difference principle—that a certain well-born and talented individual might decide to waste his talents and fortune and end up very poor.[39] Any objection based on the possibility of such a person wrongly assumes that the way to implement the difference principle is by something like cash transfers. But this is a mistake: the difference principle regulates only the background economic rules that determine the life prospects of representative individuals. It does not require that the *particular people* who end up being the poorest ought to be compensated, irrespective of their personal choices.

The difference principle is in principle compatible with a variety of social arrangements. It is a matter of social research to determine which set of taxes, market regulations, and feasible programs will in fact work to increase the lifetime expectations of the least advantaged so that they can be fully participating members of society on an equal standing with others. It is possible that certain social arrangements will maximize the lifetime expectations of the worst off in some societies but not in others, due to differences in the background culture. Moreover, social research can help design other feasible supplementary programs for those who are temporarily or permanently incapable of earning enough income to support themselves and their families.[40] Among the programs that are feasible, those that are easier to administer and that are less intrusive will be preferable. Advocating the difference principle certainly does not automatically imply endorsing the actual welfare policies of capitalist societies, and it may well turn out that the principle supports fairly radical policy requirements. In fact, Rawls claims that actual welfare capitalist societies are far from satisfying his two principles of justice, because economic and political power tends to be concentrated in such a way that the worth of political liberties is not equal and the worth of the other basic liberties is not maximized. Actual welfare capitalist societies also fall short of satisfying fair equality of opportunity and the difference principle. Rawls favors a model that he calls "property owning democracy," in which property and economic power are more widely distributed.[41] His endorsement of this model may be based on the empirical assumption that this kind of economic arrangement is the best way to secure the equal worth of the political liberties and the maximization of the worth of other basic liberties for the least advantaged.

3   Stability and Social Change

The Problem of Stability

The two principles of justice examined in the previous chapter contain the central normative prescriptions of the theory of justice as fairness. A just society—or, to use Rawls' more technical expression, a 'well-ordered society'—is one whose basic structure is effectively regulated by the two principles of justice, in the particular lexical order that has been explained. However, Rawls does not think that the set of ground rules that constitute the basic structure of society can satisfy the principles of justice in a purely mechanical way, merely in virtue of their having the right content. In particular, he does not think that the basic structure can satisfy the principles independently of the moral dispositions and commitments of citizens. Rather, the ideal of a well-ordered society implies (a) that the principles of justice are publicly known to regulate the basic structure, (b) that citizens endorse these principles as fair, and (c) that they are sufficiently motivated to behave in ways that support the maintenance of just social institutions. When these conditions are met, the principles of justice provide a shared point of view that citizens can use to adjudicate their competing claims.[1]

Because of the fact of pluralism, Rawls argues that the principles of justice can only serve their public role as a shared normative standard if they are what he calls "political principles." Part of what this means, for Rawls, is that their scope is restricted in a certain way and that they are defended on the basis of shared ideas present in the public culture of the democratic societies with which he is concerned. According to Rawls, it is only political principles, so understood, that are capable of gaining the support of citizens who have different views about the good life—views that are grounded in a variety of distinct comprehensive doctrines. One reason for this is that, as we saw in the previous chapter, political principles of justice can be thought of as forming a module that is capable of fitting with each of the different comprehensive doctrines that happen to be endorsed by citizens. Some individual citizens may of course understand the principles of justice as having a deep foundation in their particular religious, metaphysical, or moral doctrines. For example, some may think of the principles as an expression of the natural law established by God, while others may think that they are a human construction resulting from the exercise of practical reason. But it is not to be expected that any one particular deep justification of the principles will be widely shared by the citizens of a pluralistic democratic society. The principles themselves, and not their justification, can reasonably be expected to be at the focus of what Rawls calls an "overlapping consensus" among citizens who hold potentially quite different comprehensive doctrines.

After arguing that the two principles of justice can be understood as political principles in this way, Rawls introduces an interesting additional consideration in support of them: he tries to demonstrate that a society effectively regulated by these principles would be what he calls "stable." The notion of stability has significant implications for any discussion of the role that education will play in a just society, and therefore also of the role it should play in actual societies that aspire to be just. According to Rawls, considerations of stability tip the balance in favor of selecting his principles of justice in the original position, as against other alternatives. In explaining what he means by stability, Rawls asks us to think about an ideal well-ordered society that functions according to his two principles of justice, and to ask ourselves whether such a society would be capable of stably maintaining social unity and cooperation from generation to generation. We would expect the answer to this question to be 'yes,' at least if we believe that citizens who grow up under what the theory says are just social institutions would develop a sense of justice that was strong enough to give them effective motivation to comply with these institutions and support them. But Rawls' understanding of stability involves more than the mere possibility that a liberal democratic regime will endure over time. It also requires that the reasons that are publicly known to justify the structure of the constitution—and that also justify whatever policies the society has that secure equality of opportunity and the satisfaction of basic material needs—are such that citizens may be expected to endorse them.

The pluralism of democratic societies raises doubts about Rawls' claim that a well-ordered society can be stable and continue to gain the kind of free and voluntary support of its citizens over time that his theory requires. Given the fact of pluralism, we can expect that children will be educated within their families according to a variety of comprehensive doctrines.[2] In a well-ordered society that grants its citizens a wide set of liberties, there will most likely be persistent disagreement about the ultimate values that define a good life, even assuming that citizens grow up and live under just social arrangements. Now, as we have seen, considerations of stability make it important for Rawls that a significant number of citizens can be expected to acquire a sense of justice. But, even if they do, this will not be enough to ensure stability. For, since the principles of justice form a module that is merely a *part* of the set of values citizens endorse, they might very often be tempted to leave aside the requirements of justice, and to give priority to competing moral considerations that derive from their particular comprehensive doctrines. For example, stability may be threatened if a sufficiently large number of citizens, on the basis of their religious views, favor serious restrictions on the basic liberties of those who do not share their own convictions.

Reasonable Moral Psychology

Before presenting any arguments in favor of the claim that a well-ordered society regulated by the two principles of justice would be stable, it will be useful briefly to examine the account of citizenship with which Rawls is operating. Recall that, for the purposes of developing a political theory of justice, Rawls makes use of an ideal of citizens as free and equal: an ideal that he claims is implicit in the public culture of democratic societies. However, Rawls also proposes a more detailed interpretation of this ideal of free and equal citizenship, by considering the kinds of characteristics that citizens will need to have if a just society is to be possible. I will call this more detailed ideal "the ideal of a reasonable citizen." The previous chapter already described some of the features of this ideal of citizenship. As we have seen, reasonable citizens will have general rational capacities for thought, judgment, and inference, together with two specific moral capacities. These two moral capacities are (a) a capacity for a sense of justice, and (b) a capacity for a conception of the good. The first of these includes the capacity to understand and act according to just rules or principles, while the second includes the capacity to form, pursue, and perhaps eventually revise, an ordered set of goals and values that structure one's life. As has also been mentioned, each citizen is supposed to have a particular conception of the good that he or she is pursuing, which may be associated with a more or less well-articulated moral, religious, or philosophical comprehensive doctrine. Beyond these characteristics, there are two other important features of reasonable citizens that Rawls adds to complete his account. First, reasonable citizens are willing to propose and obey fair terms of social cooperation, on the condition that others do the same. And, second, reasonable citizens recognize what Rawls calls "the burdens of judgment." These "burdens" are made up of the various possible sources of disagreement regarding both factual and evaluative matters: disagreement that may persist even among people who exercise their capacities for reasoning and judgment in a careful way.

The burdens of judgment can be thought of as a set of considerations that help to explain, in the context of pluralist and democratic societies, the existence of persistent disagreement about many evaluative and factual issues, and that can also explain why this disagreement is compatible with people's correct use of their capacities for reason. Rawls holds that even when people are not blinded by self-interest, and even when they avoid reasoning in fallacious ways, they may still disagree in their judgments on a number of issues. This kind of reasonable disagreement may arise, for example, during the deliberations of a conscientious jury about whether the evidence in a particular case is sufficient to convict the accused, or during the deliberations of well-informed and sincere members of a school board about the foreseeable consequences of a proposed policy. The list of burdens of judgment that explain such disagreements include the following: the fact that the evidence about certain issues is complex and conflicting; the relative weight of different considerations may not be clear; the concepts used may be vague and there may be a number of plausible interpretations of them; the different life experiences of people may affect the ways they assess certain considerations; and there may be a number of relevant normative considerations that people can use to decide a particular case. This list might easily be expanded to include additional considerations that help explain disagreement among reasonable people. Rawls' claim that reasonable citizens accept the burdens of judgment has been subject to a number of criticisms that will be examined later. For present purposes what matters is that, in his view, reasonable citizens are capable of regarding certain disagreements about facts and normative issues as reasonable. That is, even when they are themselves parties to such disagreements, they can see them as consistent with the reasonability of those of their fellow citizens who have reached different conclusions from their own. There are of course some forms of disagreement that are not reasonable: for example, those based on ignorance, significant logical errors, or excessive self-interest or factional interest. But Rawls' argument is intended only to show that reasonable citizens could endorse the principles of justice and be sufficiently motivated to abide by them. The fact that there could be some unreasonable citizens who reject them is not strictly a problem for the stability of his theory. It is a problem in real life, which requires sensible measures to restrict its impact.

Let us return now to the question of whether a society regulated by the two principles of justice would be stable. Rawls argues that it is plausible to think that citizens who grow up in such a society will, over time, acquire the dispositions that are characteristic of reasonable citizens and that are required to maintain just institutions from generation to generation. In support of this, he argues that the characteristic features of reasonable citizens are such that most human beings can acquire them, provided they grow up in the right sort of environment. To clarify this idea, it may be useful to make a comparison. Consider for a moment a crude utilitarian principle of justice that says that all primary goods should be distributed in ways that maximize overall pleasure. This principle is consistent with a minority being denied basic rights, liberties, opportunities, and even the essential material resources for a decent life, as long as the suffering of this unfortunate minority is overbalanced by the greater pleasure of the other members of society. Let us leave aside the question of whether such a society is consistent with our reflective judgments about just social arrangements. Rather, the question of present concern is whether people who grow up in such a utilitarian society can reasonably be expected to come to freely endorse its underlying utilitarian principle and to develop the disposition to comply with it. An extremely plausible answer in this case is 'No;' it is not reasonable to anticipate that members of the unfortunate minority will come to feel that their sufferings are adequately compensated for by the greater happiness that other members of their society experience. Of course we should admit the possibility that there may be some exceptional human beings who would be willing to make great sacrifices for the sake of unknown others, and who would consistently devote their lives to the service of admirable causes. But the question is not whether such people do or could exist. Rather, it is whether it is plausible to expect most people to develop the sort of psychology that would make the utilitarian society stable. Rawls asks the same question about his two principles of justice and the kind of moral psychology that is required to support a society that is based on them. And his answer is 'Yes.' Rawls calls the required sort of moral psychology "reasonable moral psychology," and he argues that we can expect it to be widespread in the favorable conditions found in well-ordered societies.

To claim that citizens have a reasonable moral psychology is to claim, among other things, the following: (a) when citizens believe that social, political, and economic institutions are fair, they will be willing to comply with them, provided that others are willing to comply as well; (b) when other people do their part in fair arrangements, they will tend to trust them, and to respond in a fair manner; (c) trust and confidence increase when shared cooperation is sustained over time, particularly when cooperation satisfies the important interests of citizens; and (d) finally, citizens (who grow up in liberal democratic societies) will come to recognize the fact of pluralism and the burdens of judgment.[3]

In order to support claims (a), (b), and (c), Rawls refers back to an early account of the psychological development of the sense of justice in children: an account that he offered in *A Theory of Justice*. He does not give, to my knowledge, any explanation of (d). That is, he does not explain how it is that citizens will come to recognize the burdens of judgment. Perhaps he thinks that acquaintance with other citizens who seem rational and reasonable but hold very different views about the good may lead citizens, upon reflection, to accept the burdens of judgment. Now, claims (a), (b), and (c) are plausible on their own, but Rawls seems to think that they stand in need of explanation and justification. He offers an account of moral development that combines elements from different traditions of thought about the psychological basis of moral behavior.[4] Rawls' preferred story of moral development, which is inspired by the work of Jean Piaget and Lawrence Kohlberg, contains a sequence of three stages.[5] Very briefly, the stages are:

1. The morality of authority: The child grows up in a just family in which she experiences the love and affection of her parents and comes to love

and trust them in return. These feelings strengthen the disposition to respect and obey the guidelines given by her parents. At this stage, the child's proto-conception of morality consists in a set of arbitrary commands, and she is not capable of understanding more comprehensive schemes within which precepts and norms might be justified. The child desires to be like her parents and internalizes their prescriptions as standards for the evaluation of behavior. For this reason, she experiences guilt when her behavior disappoints them.

2. The morality of association: As the child matures, she participates in different associations in which social cooperation takes place. Among other associations, the family and the school are central, and a large number of cooperative regulated activities take place within them. In this way, the child learns different schemes of rights and duties, which vary with the kind of association and its level of complexity. Participation in these different associations also teaches the child to appreciate the point of view of other participants. As the child perceives the benefits of various group activities, she develops feelings of trust and friendship towards other participants, and a desire to honor her duties. She also experiences guilt when she fails to do her part in cooperative arrangements, as well as resentment when others fail to do theirs.

3. The morality of principle: The adolescent or young adult comes to understand that she and those she cares about benefit from just social institutions, and she develops an attachment to the principles of justice themselves. Once she realizes that the principles of justice promote her good and the good of others close to her, she appreciates the ideal of just cooperation and develops the desire to act according to the principles themselves in their full generality. That is, this stage involves a generalization of the sense of justice, which is what explains cooperation that is not mediated by feelings of love or friendship. On many occasions, feelings of friendship and trust come to the aid of the exercise of the personal virtue of justice. But in certain circumstances, the disposition to abide by just rules and procedures is exercised even in the absence of feelings of love and friendship towards particular people. As in early stages, feelings of guilt accompany the failure to comply with the principles of justice. It is at this stage that the sense of justice is fully developed.[6]

As Rawls himself admits, his moral psychology is quite speculative. But, perhaps surprisingly, doubts about its details, or even its broad outline, might not be very damaging to Rawls' project. For his purposes, all that is strictly necessary is that there should be some plausible story, explaining how people might come to acquire a robust disposition to apply and act upon the principles of justice.[7] In my view, the problem with this speculative account of moral development is that it is less plausible than the claims (a), (b), and (c), and is more open to empirical objections. Moreover, there is no account of the process and circumstances that lead to claim (d) about the acknowledgment of the burdens of judgment. Of course, we could not have expected Rawls to have included in *A Theory of Justice* an explanation of the way in which citizens come to appreciate the burdens of judgment. After all, the notions of reasonable disagreement and the burdens of judgment are things he added in later works. But even restricting ourselves to claims (a), (b), and (c), references to this early account of moral development give an incomplete and controversial story about the acquisition of a reasonable moral psychology. It would have been better simply to refer directly to empirical studies that have more direct bearing on the four claims.

Overlapping Consensus

As we have seen, one aspect of the problem of stability concerns the psychological plausibility of the development of the sense of justice among citizens who grow up in a well-ordered democratic society. But this is not the only problem. Citizens are also assumed to have different conceptions of the good that they are pursuing, and these conceptions may be grounded in comprehensive doctrines. This yields a second aspect of the problem of stability: an aspect that concerns the congruence between citizens' conceptions of the good and the principles of justice. For, even if we assume that all citizens have a fairly robust sense of justice, it is still a real question whether it will be strong enough to override other central motives that they may have. If the ends and values that citizens pursue—interpreted in light of the comprehensive doctrines they endorse—are often strongly at odds with the principles of justice, then we have some reason to doubt that the principles can be the basis of a just and stable regime.

Rawls' response to this second aspect of the problem of stability has changed over time. In his later works he argues that stability is possible because the principles of justice could be at the focus of an overlapping consensus of reasonable comprehensive doctrines. The idea of an overlapping consensus requires that each citizen, with her distinctive moral, religious, and philosophical view, find the module of justice as fairness acceptable in connection with her own perspective. 'Acceptable' here is to be understood in quite a strong way: the principles of justice should be compatible with important beliefs and values of citizens, and not merely accepted for reasons of strategic convenience. Ideally, the principles should find support in a citizen's core beliefs and values. But for some citizens there may be some tension between the principles of justice and certain aspects of their comprehensive doctrines. In such cases, the principles should be given priority. Rawls distinguishes the overlapping consensus from a mere *modus vivendi*: while the former implies a consensus based on moral reasons, the latter is a pragmatic agreement, and it will be unstable because it depends on a contingent convergence of interests and a balance of power. For example, members of different religious groups may agree on the state's granting religious freedom to all groups as a *modus vivendi* because no one group would have the majority allowing it to control the political process and impose its views on the rest of society. But members of these groups may be quick to suppress previously agreed upon rights to religious freedom as soon as their numbers increase and they become powerful enough to influence state policy. In contrast, an overlapping consensus on the right to free exercise of religion is a consensus based on the appropriate kinds of reasons. These need not be political or public reasons: they can be reasons grounded in particular comprehensive doctrines. What is important is that they will be reasons that would continue to exist even if the relative political power of different religious groups changed. This is because the only way that mutual trust and respect among citizens can be achieved is if basic rights are secured in way that is not subject to contingently acceptable bargains that are dependent on the balance of power among groups.

The claim that a stable theory of justice is one that could be at the focus of an overlapping consensus of comprehensive doctrines has received considerable critical attention. Moreover, it is not even clear exactly what is meant by this claim, and the obscurity has lead to a number of misinterpretations of Rawls' project. Some interpret the claim as stating that it is a condition of adequacy on the theory that there exists an actual consensus on the principles of justice in contemporary liberal democratic societies. This may seem to be an impossible condition to meet, but there is in fact significant agreement in such societies that if a society is to qualify as just, it should recognize a set of equal basic rights and liberties as belonging to all its members. Moreover, one might, at least plausibly, argue that there is a consensus on the importance of a principle of fair equality of opportunity—even though some policies inspired by this principle, such as affirmative action policies, may provoke a great deal of controversy. Unfortunately, there does not seem to be any such consensus on the difference principle, or on any similar redistributive principle. Because of a lack of actual consensus on something like the difference principle, some critics have concluded that Rawls' work has taken a conservative turn, and that he has given up on the requirements of economic justice. However, a careful reading of Rawls' later work reveals that he continues to defend the difference principle as part of his theory of justice as fairness, and as part of the overlapping consensus. This strongly suggests that Rawls was not making a pragmatic argument for his theory of justice that appealed to an existing consensus. So we should look for an alternative interpretation of the role of overlapping consensus: an interpretation that does not make the normative content of the theory dependent on the views of actual citizens.[8]

In my view, the overlapping consensus is best understood as a form of hypothetical consensus to be reached, after due deliberation, by reasonable citizens who hold reasonable comprehensive doctrines. In order to get clearer on what this means, let us begin by examining the notion of a reasonable comprehensive doctrine. Rawls defines such doctrines as having three features:

1. A reasonable doctrine is an exercise of theoretical reason: it covers the major religious, philosophical, and moral aspects of human life in a more or less consistent and coherent manner. It organizes and characterizes recognized values so that they are compatible with one another and express an intelligible view of the world.
2. In singling out which values to count as especially significant and how to balance them when they conflict, a reasonable comprehensive doctrine is also an exercise of practical reason.
3. While a reasonable comprehensive view is not necessarily fixed and unchanging, it normally belongs to, or draws upon, a tradition of thought and doctrine. Although stable over time, and not subject to sudden and unexplained changes, it tends to evolve slowly in the light of what, from its point of view, it sees as good and sufficient reasons.[9]

Rawls warns us that this definition of a reasonable comprehensive doctrine is "deliberately loose" and does not impose any significant restrictions on content. Because it is not restrictive in this way, many familiar traditional doctrines can count as reasonable. However, this loose characterization of reasonable comprehensive doctrines cannot be used as a sufficient condition for reasonability when we are selecting the doctrines that may be part of the overlapping consensus. This is because a fascist or fundamentalist comprehensive doctrine that is consistent and is integrated in a tradition would satisfy Rawls' three criteria. But it does not seem plausible to label such doctrines "reasonable." Moreover, we need not conclude that there is anything defective in the principles of justice simply because they cannot be endorsed by proponents of such doctrines.

A better strategy for interpreting the idea of an overlapping consensus makes reference to the account of "reasonable citizen" that we examined earlier. In particular, one might claim that the principles of justice could be at the focus of an overlapping consensus of reasonable doctrines (loosely defined earlier) *held by reasonable citizens.* As we have seen, reasonable citizens have a capacity for a sense of justice, which involves being willing to propose fair terms of cooperation that others could also endorse, and to act on these terms provided others do so as well. Moreover, reasonable citizens recognize the burdens of judgment and accept their consequences regarding the comprehensive doctrines that other citizens endorse, namely, that they should not be suppressed by the power of the state. If what matters for the stability of the theory is that the principles could be at the focus of an overlapping consensus among citizens who are reasonable in this sense, then doctrines that are intolerant and fail to recognize the equal rights of others do not pose any problem. Because such doctrines are not based on a morality of reciprocity and are not consistent with the disposition to propose fair terms of cooperation that others might endorse, they do not count as doctrines that reasonable citizens could possibly hold.

One might object that any argument for the stability of the principles of justice that is based on the aforementioned interpretation of the notion of overlapping consensus cannot prove anything of real interest. After all, it crucially depends on the stipulation that reasonable citizens have certain characteristics: characteristics that make it unsurprising that they give their continuing endorsement to the principles. Along these lines, some critics have argued that the ideal of a reasonable citizen is biased towards liberal views about the good life. According to one common criticism of this sort, Rawls' understanding of a reasonable citizen is too demanding because it fails to accommodate the convictions and self-understandings of some law-abiding citizens who are religious believers. The characteristic of reasonable citizens that is at the heart of this criticism is the requirement that such citizens accept the burdens of judgment and its consequences for the exercise of political power. This, according to many authors, makes problems for some religious citizens because (as per their reading) this requirement entails that citizens must adopt a skeptical or fallibilist attitude towards their own beliefs.[10] On this interpretation, accepting the burdens of judgment involves admitting the possibility that one's own convictions are mistaken. This fallibilist attitude, together with some additional premises, would then form the basis for tolerance and for an acceptance of the beliefs and ways of life of others. It would also lead one to support laws and policies only insofar as one can see them as supportable on the basis of public reasons. Critics like Leif Wenar argue that this requirement is incompatible with the ways in which a considerable number of religious believers understand their own faith, and the ways in which they interpret the existing social pluralism. Such believers see pluralism not as a result of the free exercise of reason but as an unfortunate event resulting from human weaknesses.[11]

The criticism of reasonability as implying a fallibilist attitude is a common one. But I do not think that it works. Rawls explicitly denies that the burdens of judgment imply doubts, lack of certainty, or skepticism about the value and validity of one's own comprehensive doctrine. The importance of the burdens of judgment, in my view, is that they allow one to interpret many forms of pluralism as reasonable, so that disagreement on certain normative and factual issues can be consistent with the reasonability and rationality of those who disagree. Acceptance of reasonable disagreement, in turn, induces people to make use of public reasons in political debates. Moreover, even if one did take a fallibilist attitude towards one's own view, this would not be enough to yield a tolerant attitude towards others; accepting that one could be mistaken about the truth of one's doctrine does not force one, on pain of irrationality, to adopt tolerant and respectful attitudes towards others. Criticisms of Rawls which take him to hold that reasonable citizens must embrace the pluralism that results from the burdens of judgment misfire. He does not require that everyone share the same explanation for persisting disagreement, or that they take the same attitude towards it, even if they consider it reasonable. Religious believers therefore need not admit any explanation of disagreement that is incompatible with their faith. Norman Daniels has suggested a number of distinct attitudes that reasonable people can have towards disagreement and the fact of pluralism. According to Daniels, someone who thinks there are moral truths could accept the burdens of judgment as a practical concession; as an obstacle to be overcome in the future. Someone who thinks that truth is revealed by God could think that certain truths are only transmitted to a chosen few, and that faith cannot be coerced. A third person, who, for philosophical reasons, denies that there are any moral truths, may consider pluralism a fundamental fact of moral life. In this way, accepting the burdens of judgment requires only that citizens be capable of accepting, in principle, the reasonability of others who disagree with them, and that they consider it illegitimate to use the power of the state to repress any reasonable doctrines, even those they regard as mistaken.[12]

Social Transformation

So far we have examined Rawls' arguments in support of the stability of an ideal society ordered by the two principles of justice. His claim is that such a society is stable because the principles could be at the focus of an overlapping consensus of doctrines held by reasonable citizens. However, Rawls also offers an independent argument that aims to show how a society could reach a deep and widespread moral consensus on the two principles of justice, starting from a situation of *modus vivendi*, and passing through an intermediate stage he calls "constitutional consensus." Rawls complicates matters by calling the final stage, in which there is deep and widespread moral consensus, an "overlapping consensus." But in fact, he is using two related but slightly different notions of overlapping consensus. One is the ideal consensus that ideal citizens (called reasonable citizens) could reach on the principles of justice that allows for the stability of his ideal theory of justice. The other notion, which I will call "deep and widespread moral consensus," refers to the outcome of a process that leads a significant proportion of citizens of liberal democratic societies, given favorable conditions, to come to endorse the principles of justice or other very similar principles. Rawls uses a sort of narrative in order to explain how a society could achieve a deep and widespread moral consensus on the principles of justice. The narrative he uses is interesting because it provides some clues as to how Rawls applies his ideal account of justice to non-ideal contexts. This will be relevant to the discussion in chapters 5 through to 8, which consider the kind of educational policies that might plausibly be derived from the theory of justice as fairness.

Rawls' narrative explanation begins with the assumption that at a certain historical moment different groups in conflict inside a society agree, with some reluctance, to respect certain principles of liberal justice, but merely as a *modus vivendi*. These principles are therefore incorporated into their political institutions. As time passes, however, the principles become part of the constitution that establishes procedures for elections and for passing laws, and this helps to moderate political rivalry in society. As time passes, and these liberal principles regulate the political institutions, three additional results are produced: (a) the content of certain liberties and basic political principles becomes fixed and is no longer subject to political dispute; (b) the application of these principles leads citizens to employ political arguments and use public reasons to persuade fellow citizens; and (c) political institutions that reflect liberal principles and encourage the use of public reasons promote other cooperative virtues, such as reasonability and the disposition to find agreements. When all of these results are produced, Rawls calls the general situation a *constitutional consensus*. At this point, the consensus may still lack a deep and wide basis in the comprehensive doctrines of citizens. However, the liberal principles of justice that have been incorporated in the society's political institutions will tend to generate adjustments in citizens' comprehensive doctrines, as those citizens come to accept the political procedures of a democratic government as normatively valid. This situation is different from one in which citizens accept democracy as a sort of compromise until their particular group becomes powerful enough to control the government. The step from a constitutional consensus to a deep and widespread moral consensus involves the production of a deeper and wider agreement, one that includes ideals and principles, grounded on a political theory of justice, that regulates the basic structure of society.

When precisely does Rawls think that a deep and widespread moral consensus (which he misleadingly also calls "an overlapping consensus") is achieved in a particular society? One requirement is that there be substantial agreement among actual citizens on certain "constitutional essentials" and provisions of basic justice, and that these essential provisions be incorporated into the law. The relevant provisions are: (a) fundamental principles that specify the general structure of government and the political process: the powers of the legislature, executive, and the judiciary; the scope of majority rule; and (b) equal basic rights and liberties of citizenship that legislative majorities are to respect: such as the right to vote and to participate in politics, liberty of conscience, freedom of thought and association, as well as the protections of the rule of law.[13]

Rawls adds that the essential provisions also include some principle of equality of opportunity and the guarantee of a social minimum that ensures that citizens can meet their basic needs. But these last two principles need not take exactly the form of his second principle of justice.[14] This acknowledgment does not imply that he is giving up on the second principle, or denying that it is supported by the strongest reasons. Rawls is simply speculating about how a deep and widespread moral consensus on principles of social justice could be generated. And he acknowledges that policies that are designed to guarantee equal opportunities and resources to citizens will not necessary match his second principle in all its detail. But he still thinks that such policies must include sufficiently similar provisions if a society is to count as just.

Rawls' narrative about the origins of a deep and widespread moral consensus on the principles of justice (or similar principles) emphasizes the importance of developing a tradition of tolerance and commitment to the exercise of public reason. It is worth noting that he appeals to some sort of mechanical socio-historical processes that results in a convergence on the right political values. In the working-out of these processes, shared political institutions play a non-intentional educational role; living under just political arrangements leads to the widespread acceptance of the principles of justice and generates some motivation to comply with them. But this explanation completely ignores the fact that more self-conscious efforts to bring about social transformation may be essential to the production of a deep and wide consensus on the principles of justice. The narrative that Rawls offers appeals to something like an invisible hand. By itself this is too optimistic. Moreover, it does not seem to appreciate the need for deliberate educational efforts to develop and sustain consensus on basic aspects of democratic government and on social policy. As we will see in chapter 5, Rawls offers only very brief comments on the role of educational institutions; he says only that schools should teach future citizens about their rights and duties, and encourage political virtues.[15] But these brief remarks are hard to reconcile with his claims about the importance of the stability of the principles of justice, which requires that citizens develop their capacities for reasonability. Rawls' theory needs to be supplemented by a more substantial account of the role of educational institutions.

4   The Family

The Variety of Family Forms

Rawls claims that the family is one of the institutions that form the basic structure of society. But he does not provide any sustained discussion of the family, as he does in the case of the other institutions that form the basic structure. This is something of a disappointment, since the institution of the family raises a number of interesting methodological and normative issues for the theory of justice as fairness. Some of these issues have significant educational implications. One important point of this chapter will be to shed some light on these implications. But before turning to this topic there is a preliminary question that needs to be addressed: what, from the perspective of a Rawlsian account of justice, should we count as a family? Theorists of justice often assume that families take a particular limited form, and consequently, the policies they propose often turn out to be too limited to be adequate for the existing variety of family forms. In particular, discussions of the moral and political status of the family tend to presuppose that it is constituted by a heterosexual (married) couple and one or more children who have biological ties to the couple, or who have been legally adopted by the couple, all of whom live together in the same home. Sometimes a traditional division of labor is also assumed to hold between the adult members of the family, with the male's primary responsibility being to provide for the family income and the female's primary responsibility being to care for the children and do the housework. Thinking about families on the basis of these kinds of assumptions fails to take into account the existence of single-parent families, families whose adult members are gay or lesbian couples, families made up of couples who have divorced but who continue to share the legal custody and care of their children (and who may have remarried and may also live with the children of their new partners), as well as larger extended families, the members of which live together in the same household.[1]

One problem that results from working with a restricted model of the family is that doing so might seem to pass judgment on family forms that deviate from one's preferred description. Although the topics discussed in this chapter tend to apply primarily to families headed by a pair of hetero-sexual adults who are raising children, some of the same problems raised by this particular type of family will apply to other types of families as well. Moreover, this chapter is not meant to provide a comprehensive examination of the issues that different kinds of families raise for theories of justice. The majority of families do not fit the simple two-parent, single home model, and this fact has important consequences for the fair distributions of benefits and burdens of cooperation among citizens in existing pluralist democratic societies. Many of these consequences are consequences for the adult members of families who have to combine paid work with the unpaid work of caring for children. But family forms also have a very significant impact on children. In particular, families make an important difference to children's access to the essential goods that are necessary for them to be able to live good lives, both in the present and as future adults. For example, children's access to a wide variety of educational goods is affected as much or more by the kinds of families they belong to, as by the kinds of educational and social policies existing in the societies in which they are raised.[2]

But to return to the issue of how we should understand what the family is, Colin Macleod has proposed a useful definition that avoids the problems that come with an overly restrictive understanding:

> The affective family is a social group comprised by one or more adults and one or more children who are linked together by a special history (for example, as biological kin or adoption) and by sentiments of mutual affection. Some of the adults in such a group have a socially and legally recognized status as parents or guardians that confers upon them a special measure of authority over and responsibility for the children in the group.[3]

This definition is particularly useful in the present context because it is wide enough to include a variety of family forms. It is true that Macleod's definition requires that the adult members of a group have children in order to count as a family. This restriction may be important for some purposes, since in some contexts we may wish to think of a pair of adults with a long-term affective relationship as constituting a family, even if they do not have (or no longer have) children. But our present concern is the effects of families on children's education, and a number of related issues that families with children raise for the theory of justice as fairness. As a consequence, this restrictive aspect of Macleod's definition will not have any distorting effects on our discussion.

In his early work Rawls gives the strong impression that he is assuming a very traditional model of family, one that not only has two parents, but that also involves a gendered division of labor. The description of the original position in that early work referred to the parties that select the principles of justice as "heads of families." Moreover, the account of moral development in *A Theory of Justice* included references to the roles of husband, wife, son, and daughter.[4] This suggested that he took families to be made up of heterosexual couples and their biological or adopted children, and that he was thinking of the roles of family members—even of children—as assigned on the basis of their sex. But in response to feminist criticisms of these early remarks about the family, Rawls made it explicit that he was not presupposing any particular family form, or any particular arrangement for the division of benefits and burdens within the family.[5] But he does insist, without offering any argument or explanation of precisely what he means, that "the family in some form" is a just social institution. The present chapter will try to shed some light on this claim.

It is worth mentioning that, given his focus on ideal theory, Rawls does not consider the problem of unjust, highly dysfunctional, or abusive families. The existence of such families in non-ideal societies requires specific public responses designed to prevent or mitigate the damage they might otherwise cause to their members, especially to the most vulnerable ones. But Rawls' theory does not aim to provide guidelines for these kinds of situations of noncompliance with basic requirements of justice. Rather, his main concern is to provide and to argue for a model of a just society, which contains just families.

Do the Principles of Justice Apply to the Family?

Although Rawls explicitly includes the family as part of the basic structure of society, he denies that the principles of justice apply *directly* to the family. This denial might seem puzzling, or it might give the impression that, for Rawls, families have some special exemption from the basic constraints of justice. However, what Rawls says about the subject of justice as fairness provides the basis for a more plausible interpretation of his remarks. As has already been stressed, the primary subject of justice for Rawls is the basic structure, which consists of a system of major social institutions. It is true that the principles of justice determine what counts as a fair distribution of social primary goods. But these principles classify a society as just as long as the *set of major social institutions*, taken as a functioning unit, ensures such a fair distribution. This does not mean that each major social institution must (or even can) satisfy both principles of justice on its own. Rather, it only means that its interrelated functioning with the other institutions results in the satisfaction of the principles of justice.[6]

Admittedly, all social institutions must respect the basic rights and liberties of citizens. This fact gives some minimal sense to the claim that the first principle of justice applies directly to all social institutions. But of course in this sense it also applies to associations and even to individual citizens. What, then, is the special relationship that the major social institutions have with the first principle? I would suggest the following: it is the legal and political institutions that distribute equal rights and liberties. That is, these are the institutions that assign and guarantee equal basic rights and liberties to all citizens. For example, I can only say that I have a right to vote if the law in a particular society allows me to vote. Of course individuals and associations must not prevent me from exercising this right. But whether or not they do, I still *have* the right. Moreover, the right to political liberty, which includes the right to vote, does not imply that associations should always be organized in a democratic way. Similar remarks can be made for other basic rights, such as the right to practice one's religion, or the right to express one's views. So we should distinguish the requirement to *respect* basic rights and liberties from the requirement to *ensure* certain rights and liberties. It is the second requirement that finds expression in the first principle of justice, and this principle applies directly only to certain major institutions: those with legal authority to grant formal rights.

Regarding the second principle of justice, even a little thought should make it clear that it cannot be necessary that each separate social institution satisfies the two parts of this complex principle. For example, families do not need to distribute resources according to the principle of fair equality of opportunity. In fact, it does not even make sense to expect that families should do this. In order to satisfy the second principle it is necessary to create fair background social conditions for access to desirable jobs and positions of authority, making sure that those who are born into the least advantaged social positions have life prospects similar to those of people who are born into more advantaged positions. Families simply cannot do this. One might try to apply the principle "internally" to the family, and say that families should distribute goods in such a way that their members have similar life chances (provided they are equally talented and motivated). But while in larger societies there can be groups of similarly talented and motivated individuals, the same generally is not true within a family. Moreover, the life prospects of a family member are going to be significantly affected by the generation to which that member belongs. In the case of adults, their prospects will be affected by earlier decisions about what kind of jobs and lifestyles to pursue. We could try to avoid these problems by focusing on children: the benefits they receive from their families, and how these benefits will affect their life chances. But this strategy is useless when thinking about families with only one child. And even in the case of families with two or more children, if we compare the benefits that children receive, and the results for their life prospects, we would not be using Rawls' principle of fair equality of opportunity. Rather, we would be employing some principle of fair consideration of the interests of children.

Accepting that we cannot apply the principle of fair equality of opportunity directly to the institution of the family is not the same as ignoring the fact that families have a significant impact on the life prospects of their members. For adults, families have this impact by virtue of the way in which paid work, domestic tasks, and care for children are allocated. For children, families have this impact by virtue of the education that they make available, both within the family and by means of the access they provide to schools and other educational resources, such as museums, theaters, camps, travel, and so on. Some families are very supportive of their children's development of intellectual capacities and marketable skills, while others are not. Rawls acknowledges that these differences in the internal functioning of families may have unfair consequences regarding the life prospects and opportunities of children. For this reason, the satisfaction of fair equality of opportunity requires social policies that compensate for such differences. For instance, there should be programs in schools that are designed to reduce the achievement gap between students from different family backgrounds.

Let us turn now to consider the difference principle, and its possible application to the family. Obviously, the adult members of a family do have a responsibility to make sure that the important needs of all members are satisfied, if they can. But, despite the claims of some of Rawls' critics, this is not equivalent to a requirement that the distribution of resources within the family should be in accord with the difference principle. Strictly speaking, the difference principle is characterized by Rawls as a principle of reciprocity that applies only to adults who are working for a salary. In my view, this understanding of the difference principle has significant shortcomings because it fails to take into account the socially indispensable but unpaid work of caring for children, as well as for sick or disabled family members.[7] But we can leave this worry aside for the moment, since even if the difference principle were amended to recognize the work of caring for children and other family members, it would remain true that it cannot apply directly to the family. The difference principle requires that the life prospects of access to income and wealth (and other social primary goods) of the least advantaged working members of society are maximized, understanding 'least advantaged' to refer to those with the fewest marketable skills. Members of a family, including an extended family, may support each other and help each other to satisfy their needs. But the consequences of this sort of family solidarity are not necessarily that the prospects of the worst-off members of society are always maximized. In some cases, the fact that family members help each other may have as its most significant result the improved prospects of the better-off members of society. For example, wealthy parents can purchase homes for their adult children, or can transfer part of their wealth to them. Again, one might try to apply the principle "internally," and say that inequalities in primary goods should benefit the worst-off members of a family. The main difficulty with this proposal is in defending a useful interpretation of 'worst-off.' Children are certainly the most vulnerable members of a family, but being most vulnerable is not the same as being worst-off. Depending on circumstances, children's life prospects (measured in terms of life expectations of access to primary goods) may be much better than those of their parents.

One might wonder why families are included as part of the basic structure, since they do not strictly satisfy the two parts of the second principle of justice. But in fact we have just seen that *no* institution, by itself, can be taken to do this. Despite this, there are still reasons to wonder why Rawls includes the family as part of the basic structure. Indeed, he sometimes compares families to associations such as churches or clubs, which do not form part of the basic structure, and whose functioning is constrained by the principles of justice only in the minimal sense that they should not violate the rights, liberties, and opportunities of their members. But there are many important differences between such associations and the family. Provided that membership is truly voluntary and that there is a background of just social arrangements, associations are allowed a wide variety of rules for their internal functioning. In contrast with the voluntary membership characteristic of associations, only the relationship between the adult members of a family is voluntary.[8] The relationship between parent and child is voluntary on the side of the parent only. And the remaining family relations are entirely non-voluntary. That is, we cannot voluntarily choose our parents, siblings, cousins, or step-parents. The non-voluntary nature of many family relationships, and the importance of the goods that are provided by the family, make it significantly different from voluntary associations.

Rawls does offer one explicit reason for including the family among the major social institutions of the basic structure; he appeals to its essential function in establishing "the orderly production and reproduction of society and of its culture from one generation to the next."[9] In contemporary democratic societies, families play by far the most significant role in the raising of children. In particular, the early moral development of children and their initiation into a particular culture depends on families. In this sense, the family is an institution with deep effects on citizens' life prospects, and on their characters and goals, and this explains its inclusion in the basic structure. Véronique Munoz-Dardé has pointed out that Rawls does not pause to consider the possibility that alternative social arrangements for rearing and educating children might be more efficient and effective in helping a society as a whole to satisfy the principles of justice.[10] For example, he does not compare raising children in families with the system used in kibbutzim, or with compulsory state-run boarding schools. Rawls' failure to consider such alternatives may be due to the fact that the idea of abolishing the family as we know it seems to be a violation of adults' basic liberties to live with and raise their children according to their values. And it is very plausible that these basic liberties may permissibly be restricted only when the important interests of children are not being satisfied. Moreover, and perhaps more importantly, Rawls seems to assume that families are generally the best institutional arrangement to satisfy the important interests of children. In fact, Rawls' account of the development of the sense of justice proceeds precisely on the basis of something like this idea.

However, even in Rawls' well-ordered society, families may have sub-optimal effects on the development of children's capacities and on the opportunities and resources available to them. This is because acceptable variations in family structure, functioning, and values will unavoidably result in unequal life chances. Even Rawls' ideal theory requires a number of compensating policies for these permissible family differences. But the application of the theory to non-ideal societies requires that even more attention be paid to the development of policies for dealing with the existence of unjust families, as well as supportive and caring families that simply cannot provide their children with all the resources and attention that they need.

Another justification that is available to Rawls for the inclusion of families in the basic structure is one that appeals to their distributive functions. Families have an impact on the distribution of the benefits and burdens of social cooperation among adults, as well as on the benefits that children receive. One might plausibly argue that the important distributive functions played by families are themselves enough to recommend their inclusion in the basic structure. One central topic in discussions of social justice would then concern the ways in which the distributive effects of families can be balanced by the effects of other social institutions so that the basic structure as a whole satisfies the two principles of justice. However, Rawls does not argue along these lines in order to justify the inclusion of the family in the basic structure. Nor, in fact, does he give any sustained consideration to the distributive effects of families. In the section entitled 'The Distributive Functions of Families and Children's Education' we will explore some of the issues that the distributive effects of families raise, as they impact on children's access to educational resources. But before discussing issues regarding the family that Rawls does *not* consider, it will be worthwhile to become more familiar with some of the issues that he *does* address. One of these is the role of the family as 'the first school of justice.'

The First School of Justice

In chapter 3 we briefly discussed Rawls' account of moral development.[11] According to this account, the family plays a key function as the first school of justice. During the developmental stage characterized by acceptance of a morality of authority, children learn the first norms in the context of their families. The love and support of a child's parents not only generate a desire to be like them and to imitate their behavior, but also play a crucial role in the internalization of corresponding norms. During the stage of the morality of association, children learn and accept rules for the distribution of responsibilities among family members, partly because they can perceive that these rules promote their own good and the good of other members of the family. The content of the morality of association comes from the particular standards attached to the variety of roles in the associations in which children participate. Children take part in other associations outside the family, such as school groups, sports teams, and groups of peers with whom they play games. These activities are structured by different rules and teach them about a variety of ways to cooperate with others on fair terms. But families continue to be one of the most significant influences during the acquisition of the role-based morality that is characteristic of this intermediate stage in moral development.

Susan Moller Okin has argued that the role of families in the moral development of children gives rise to a serious internal tension in Rawls' theory. A central issue for Okin is that the principles of justice do not apply directly to the internal life of families but families are nevertheless required to be just so that they can support the moral development of children.[12] Okin agrees with Rawls that the stability of a just society crucially depends on the acquisition of the sense of justice that starts in the context of the family. It is in the context of their families that children first acquire a sense of themselves, of their rights and duties, and of their relations to others. But according to Okin, if the principles of justice do not apply to the family, family justice is not guaranteed and the stability of a just society cannot, consequently, be secured.

Okin's criticism of Rawls and the function he assigns to families in children's moral development focuses on families in which the adults are a heterosexual couple.[13] Her claim is that the internal functioning of many of these families violates norms of equal concern and respect. The power to make decisions in the family is often not shared equally between husband and wife, because such power tends to be correlated with earning power and many wives are financially dependent on their husbands. Moreover, the work that husband and wife do is generally not equally valued (this happens when one is paid and the other one is unpaid, or one is paid significantly more than the other), or is not fairly distributed (this happens when both husband and wife have paid jobs, but most of the domestic work is done by the wife). Okin argues that when the relationship between the adult members of a family is not based on reciprocity and equal consideration, but on domination and exploitation, it is unlikely that children will come to learn fair and egalitarian norms.

According to Okin, in many families the education that girls and boys receive in crucial formative years tends to perpetuate stereotypes about gender roles that assign differential entitlements and responsibilities to family members on the basis of their sex.[14] Following empirical studies, Okin argues that an unequal division of labor between husband and wife tends to be correlated with an unequal contribution to housework by adolescent sons and daughters. And this suggests that "patterns of family injustice" are typically passed on from generation to generation.[15] Widespread acceptance of stereotyped gender roles, in turn, negatively affects the exercise of liberties, the opportunities, and the access to resources of women in contemporary democratic societies. Okin argues that, because women are perceived as primarily responsible for rearing children, and the job market is structured on the assumption that serious workers do not also have the responsibility of rearing children, women's opportunities and access to economic resources are unfairly limited. Okin's conclusion is that a society cannot satisfy the principles of justice unless, among other things, the internal life of families is significantly transformed. For this reason, she recommends a number of public policies that encourage men and women to share both paid work and domestic tasks, including the care of children. Because some families will continue to divide responsibilities for paid work and domestic work along more traditional lines, Okin also proposes additional policies that are designed to protect stay-at-home mothers (or fathers) and their children, who may be seriously disadvantaged in the event of divorce.

At the heart of Okin's criticism of Rawls is the claim that a refusal to apply the principles of justice to the internal functioning of families undermines the stability of the theory of justice as fairness. Let us assess this claim. We have already explained that, for Rawls, the principles apply to the set of major institutions of the basic structure as a whole. As we have noted, this does not entail that families are internally opaque to *any* requirements of justice. Rather, it means that just norms or just decisions concerning family life have to be appropriate to the kind of institution that the family is.[16] Rawls' two principles of justice were not designed to be applied directly to family life. Rather, he intended them to apply to the basic structure of society. Rawls would agree with Okin's general claim that if children grow up in (seriously) unjust families, they will have difficulties in developing their moral capacities and in attaining a mature sense of justice or a reasonable conception of the good. However, Rawls and Okin disagree on the standards according to which a distribution of tasks in the family counts as just or not.[17] Rawls' theory makes room for a variety of conceptions of reasonably just family arrangements. In particular, he does not hold that the fairest family arrangement is one in which adults do roughly equal amounts of paid, domestic, and childcare work. Because justice as fairness aims to make room for a number of permissible conceptions of the good, it cannot advocate any very specific conception of fair family arrangements, since this is a topic about which there are disagreements among reasonable citizens.[18] Rawls' theory will refrain from negatively assessing traditional arrangements for the division of labor inside the family, just as long as they are entered into voluntarily and are not accepted as a result of the constraints of circumstances (for example, because there is no adequate childcare in the area, or because the paid jobs that are available are not flexible enough to be compatible with childcare responsibilities). Rawls' latitude on this issue cannot be condemned as turning a blind eye to injustices that occur inside the family, since he will still rule out abuse, coercion, exploitation, and manipulation as unjust. Moreover, he agrees with Okin that men should not be allowed to exit a marriage without a continuing obligation to share their income with their ex-wives and children.[19]

In my view, Okin's claim that there is a serious flaw in the theory of justice because the two principles do not apply directly to the family is based on a misreading of the scope of the principles. One might attempt to reformulate her criticism by claiming that justice as fairness cannot be stable unless it includes the requirement that families satisfy a strictly egalitarian conception of family justice. This modified version of Okin's criticism admits that principles of justice for the basic structure of society may take a different form from the principles of family justice. However, to support this reformulated criticism, one would need to show one of the following two things: (a) that only families in which adults share paid, domestic, and childcare work are just, so that allowing other family arrangements would involve condoning injustice; or (b) that other family arrangements, while they are not in themselves unjust, nevertheless reliably function to undermine the background justice of society.

The problem with (a) is that it conflicts with many people's considered judgments about fair family arrangements, and seems to prescribe a very limited range of forms that the internal distribution of tasks can acceptably take. Okin's ideal of a just society is that of a society "without gender." According to Okin, gender is the deeply entrenched social institutionalization of sexual difference. So the ideal society she has in mind would have no distinction between the roles that men and women play. This ideal certainly seems inconsistent with the idea that at least some family arrangements based on a gendered division of labor are reasonably just. In her own words:

> Rawls does not explain the basis of his assumption that family institutions are just. If gendered families are *not* just, but are, rather, a relic of caste or feudal societies in which roles, responsibilities and resources are distributed not in accordance with the principles of justice but in accordance with innate differences that are imbued with enormous social significance, then Rawls' whole structure of moral development would seem to be built on shaky ground. [...] How, in hierarchical families in which sex roles are rigidly assigned, are we to learn, as Rawls' theory of moral development requires us to, to "put ourselves into another's place and find out what we would do in his position?" Unless they are parented equally by adults of both sexes, how will children of both sexes come to develop a sufficiently similar and well-rounded moral psychology to enable them to engage in the kind of deliberation about justice that is exemplified in the original position?[20]

Okin also holds that those arrangements in which husband and wife do paid work, but in which the wife does a "second shift" of domestic and childcare work are even more unjust.[21] This type of arrangement is plausibly more exploitative and unfair than one in which husband and wife do roughly the same amount of work but in which the kind of work each one does is based on a gendered division of labor. Okin would probably insist that these latter arrangements count as unjust because the kind of work each spouse does is generally not equally valued. Moreover, such arrangements tend to be correlated with less decision-making power for women inside the marriage and diminished opportunities for women in the future.

Let us now turn to claim (b). This claim is easier to defend when one considers the widespread and systematic division of labor based on gender that characterizes most societies. The idea behind (b) is that if a high proportion of women opt out of the labor market or take badly paid part-time jobs, there will be less pressure in society to accommodate the needs of full-time working women and their partners who are raising children. This would make it more difficult for couples who want to combine paid and childcare work. Moreover, if a high proportion of women choose to become stay-at-home mothers, this is likely to reinforce widespread stereotypes that assume that women are not interested in or qualified for certain kinds of professional jobs, or that they are likely to opt out of the labor market when they have children. Although I agree that these are some of the likely consequences of a widespread preference for a traditional division of labor in families, one problematic aspect of this argument for (b) is that the effects of family arrangements on social justice are difficult to separate from the effects of other social institutions and policies.[22] If we take the aforementioned considerations as merely providing an instrumental argument against a gendered division of labor inside the family, then whether or not this arrangement counts as unjust will be contingent on its effects in a particular society. As Okin herself has persuasively shown, women's opportunities, access to resources, and the worth of their liberties do not depend *only* on family arrangements. Rather, they also depend significantly on whether or not there are social policies that take into account the fact that many workers are raising children and that families need more resources than single individuals if they are going to be able to satisfy the important needs of their members.[23] I think that the decision to divide labor along traditional lines in families has, for many couples, much more to do with the current structure of the labor market, the availability of affordable childcare, and the length of school hours, among other things, than with a choice that expresses the unconstrained preferences of women (and men).[24] In my view, if social polices were set up to better accommodate the needs of working parents and to make the working environment more hospitable to women, it would be very unlikely that traditional divisions of labor would continue to be as widespread, or that such a high percentage of women with children would end up in jobs that do not pay very well. So although it is true that a widespread traditional division of labor tends to perpetuate social injustice, it is not clear to me that decisions about family life are the main cause of this unjustice. Changing social conditions and the costs of certain career options may very well be enough to change the actual choices that couples make, and social expectations about women's work.[25]

In contrasting the views of Rawls and Okin, one interesting issue that arises concerns the need—or the lack of a need—for significant congruence between the principles that regulate the internal workings of the family and the principles that regulate the basic structure of society. In other words, the question arises as to whether such congruence is necessary if families are to be capable of positively supporting the moral and political education of children. Rawls' view is that there is a range of fair family arrangements, associated with a corresponding range of different conceptions of the good that adult citizens might reasonably hold. As a result, there is a discontinuity between the rules of fairness for families on the one hand, and principles of justice for the basic structure of society on the other. Okin might object to this aspect of Rawls' view by claiming that the resulting discontinuity will prevent families from functioning as true schools of justice. But it is not clear how much congruence one can expect between institutional structures that are as different from one another as the basic structure of society and the family. Moreover, we should consider what is really required for children to be able to develop their sense of justice and a reasonable conception of the good. One thing that clearly matters is that both girls and boys receive enough love, support, and encouragement to acquire a secure sense of themselves and of their equal rights. It also matters that they learn to be properly responsive to the claims and needs of others, that they develop a sense of fairness, a capacity to see the points of view of other people, and to compromise in order to resolve disputes. Families that fail to teach these core political values are inadequate schools of justice since they may make it easier for children, when they grow up, to form relationships of domination and servility.[26] But families that do teach the core political values may be doing all that can reasonably be required of them. Of course it should be clear by now that the accommodation of a range of reasonable conceptions of family life does not imply that parents should have unlimited authority to raise their children in any way they want. But there can be a fairly extensive latitude for parents, provided that other social institutions supplement the moral and political education that families provide.

Because families are not the only institutions or associations in which children, adolescents, and adults will participate, Rawls' theory requires only that certain *threshold* moral capacities be adequately nurtured specifically in the family.[27] Participation in other social institutions and associations is required to supplement children's moral and political education. This is true for a number of reasons, many of which stem from the obvious fact that families cannot adequately mirror the diversity and complexity of contemporary democratic societies.[28] These reasons help explain why the education that children receive at schools is an essential supplement to family education: schools provide a more diverse environment, in which children are required to interact with adults and children who are not family members. In this way, children have greater opportunity to become aware of alternative conceptions of the good, including alternative ways of structuring family life. Awareness of this kind of diversity is essential if children are to acquire the dispositions characteristic of reasonable citizens. Moreover, schools should teach children about the structure of the political and legal systems, and about the rights and responsibilities of citizens, since this information is often not imparted fully (or even partially) by parents. With all this in mind, what Rawls' theory expects from families is that they provide a threshold level of development of the capacities for reasonable citizenship. Other social institutions can supplement this task, so there is no need for the principles that operate within just families to be congruent with the principles of wider social justice. Of course, some families do fail to provide this threshold level of development of moral and political capacities. This might happen if the children enter adulthood without having acquired sufficient concern for other people's interests, points of view, or reasonable claims. Alternately, it might happen if the children grow up without learning to appreciate their own equal moral status and the validity of certain claims they can make against others members of society. Families in which either of these things happen certainly fail as schools of justice as per Rawls' approach.

To recapitulate briefly, Rawls includes the family as part of the basic structure of society because it serves essential functions with respect to both the care and education of children. Rawls thinks that the healthy moral and emotional development of children requires a close and loving relationship with at least one adult, and that this justifies the existence of the institution of the family. Because, according to his theory, a just society should provide a framework within which citizens can pursue their reasonable conceptions of the good, he refuses to endorse any particular conception of fairness in family arrangements. Rawls claims that there are some basic requirements of justice that the relationships between family members must satisfy (many of which should be enforced by law). But his theory proceeds on the assumptions that family members are united by feelings of love and concern for each other, that families will find fair and agreed-upon ways of distributing tasks and resources, and that children will be properly cared for in the context of their families. All of this is focused at the level of ideal theory and Rawls does not even try to address the problem of seriously unjust families. For those who wish to develop policy recommendations for non-ideal contexts, it is important to keep in mind that sensible policies will have to take into account the existence not only of loving and supportive families, but of significantly dysfunctional families and families that fall somewhere between these two extremes.

The Distributive Functions of Families and Children's Education

Families do much more than merely provide for the care and education of children: they also have a number of distributive functions. Adults who do paid work are often members of families, and if so they are generally inclined (and expected) to share their income with the other members of the family. Because of this, even if a theory of justice does not provide a conception of fair family arrangements, it must still take into account the redistributive effects of the existence of families. One interesting methodological issue faced by theories of justice and by empirical studies of social inequality concerns the resulting problem of how to understand income distribution.[29] When assessing the justice of income distribution in a particular society it makes a great deal of difference whether one looks at individual income or at household income, and whether or not one factors in the number of so-called 'dependents' in a household. Feminists have rightly pointed out that a focus on household income as the unit of analysis tends to obscure the fact that there are often significant differences between the earning capacities of adults in a family. These differences, in turn, tend to have an influence on a number of further matters: on the decision-making power of the adults inside the family, on the amount of domestic and childcare work each adult does, and on the life prospects of each in the event of divorce. But the alternative focus—on individual income—also seems problematic. For example, someone who makes no income or a low income should not necessarily be counted among the worst off, because she or he may be a member of a wealthy family and have abundant access to all sorts of resources (at least until divorce, or until the wealthy relative decides to be less generous). On the other hand, someone else may make an income that is more than sufficient to cover her own economic needs, but this may not be nearly enough to provide sufficiently for her dependents.

Other difficulties concerning the distributive aspects of families have to do with what children themselves are owed as a matter of justice. It seems intuitively correct to say that adults who earn an income (under fair conditions) are entitled to share it with their family. But, in the absence of policies that function to mitigate the impact of this kind of family partiality, allowing people to share their income with family members has as a result the life prospects of children being largely determined by family background (or as Rawls calls it, the social lottery). The children of wealthier families will have access to far more resources than children of poorer families. This disparity is likely to result in unfair advantages for some children, and in unfair disadvantages for others. Thus, there is a clear tension between the freedom of adults to share their income with their families and the rights of children to fair life prospects.[30]

Does Rawls' theory of justice have the tools required to deal with this tension? Rawls sometimes writes as if the principles of justice were only meant to solve problems of distribution of goods among adults. But there is a plausible interpretation of the deliberations of the parties in the original position that may be useful for our purposes: parties should take into account the fact that once the veil is lifted they may be representing a child who has a family with limited resources. If the parties are interested in securing the life prospects of individuals' access to resources, then they will try to make sure that availability of certain fundamental goods is not dependent on the family's capacity to pay for them.[31] Or, to put the point in slightly different terms, a plausible description of the original position will take into account that during part of their lives human beings are children. In my view, taking this fact into account in the original position does not make it necessary to modify the content of the principles of justice chosen there. But the correct implementation of the principles must pay adequate heed to the fact that some of the beneficiaries of the principles are children. In practice the satisfaction of the principles of justice will require that the distributive functions of families are regulated (by taxation and redistributive policies) in such a way that children's access to important resources does not rely on their families' income but is publicly guaranteed. Colin Macleod argues that there are specific goods that children need in order to live good lives *as children*. He criticizes existing theories of justice because, insofar as they consider children at all, they adopt a prospective approach to justice that looks only at the future opportunities and resources that children will have as adults. He is right on this point: Rawls' social primary goods do not properly capture the kinds of goods that children need to live good lives. For example, young children do not need political liberties and income since they are not mature enough to make decisions about how to use them. Macleod proposes that the basic resources children require are the following: education, health care, nutritious food, shelter, a loving family, and opportunities to play. It is helpful to take these goods into account when thinking about the sorts of things that public policies should make accessible. For example, Macleod argues that leisure and recreational opportunities should be available for children as a matter of justice, in the form of community centers, public parks, and so on.

However, the same considerations that have traditionally led Rawlsians to allow for some permissible inequalities among adults will continue to hold. That is, a certain amount of social inequality is permissible as long as it provides an incentive structure that results in more goods being available for everyone, including the worst off.[32] Given that children will be raised in families, the theory of justice as fairness therefore seems committed to accept as permissible at least *some* inequalities among children.

What does the theory of justice have to say about the funding of education and the criteria for the distribution of educational goods? Although this is a topic that requires a great deal of additional discussion, it is worth sketching the kind of response that seems most consistent with Rawls' theory. We have already discussed the fact that a significant portion of a child's education takes place in a family, and that there are reasons to support raising children in families, even if this results in inequalities among children. But an equally significant portion of a child's education takes place in school, and this portion can be subject to public regulation and control without jeopardizing the important functions of families. Moreover, admitting that families play a fundamental role in the healthy moral and psychological development of children, or that parents are entitled to share their income with their children by no means requires us to condone the existing effects of family partiality in most societies. This is because the distribution of desirable social positions and income in most societies is far from fair, and does not satisfy the requirements of both parts of the second principle of justice. If a parent has an unfairly high income, it perpetuates injustice to allow that parent to will all her wealth to her children, or to spend it in ways that perpetuate social injustices.

Using a Rawlsian framework, one might be tempted to focus on the fair equality of opportunity principle to shed some light on the question of how education should be distributed to children. But for a Rawlsian this is not the right principle to begin with, and in my view it should not be the main principle we appeal to when making decisions about the distribution of educational goods for children.[33] Rather, we should begin with the principle of equal liberty, since it has lexical priority over fair equality of opportunity. Although this first principle of justice is not directly applicable to children, since they are not mature enough to enjoy their liberties, a reasonable application of the principle would recommend that children receive an education that prepares them to form and pursue their own conception of the good and to make use of their rights and liberties in the future. The worth of children's future liberties can only be maximized if they manage to develop a variety of talents that they can later use to select and pursue a valuable plan of life. Thus, children's education should be designed largely by taking into account their future status as equal citizens, and their resulting current interest in developing and pursuing their own conception of the good. This means that children's education should enable them to become competent to participate in a variety of social institutions and associations, including the political system and the labor market.[34] These kinds of considerations support a well-funded state-mandated education for all children from primary through to high school. One central goal of such an education should be the achievement of a relatively high threshold level of relevant competences, independently of family background, talent, motivation, and skill.[35]

It is true that children have different natural talents, interests, and motivations. Even under the most effective policies designed to compensate for these differences, the result will be that they will reach different levels of educational achievement. Further, these educational differences will express themselves in differential social and economic prospects. But it would be a mistake to focus all of our attention on the resulting issues of fair equality of opportunity, especially in primary and secondary education. Education serves more purposes than merely preparing children for competition for desirable social positions in the future. As Harry Brighouse has pointed out, there are a number of 'intrinsic goods' that education provides and that children must be acquainted with in order to, later on, choose a plan of life and become fully participating members of society.[36] Acquaintance with these intrinsic goods is acquired as one learns to entertain, execute, and reflect on a variety of tasks, such as reading books, playing musical instruments, building things, cooking food, and so on. Learning to perform at least some of these tasks and to enjoy at least some of these kinds of goods is required if children are to be able to develop their own conception of the good life and to make use of their liberties. Moreover, some relatively substantial knowledge of the workings of the legal and political system is also required if children are to make effective use of their future legal and political rights. This is necessary to secure the fair value of their political liberties, as required by the first principle of justice.

In terms of educational policy, taking seriously the ideal of equal citizenship favors equalizing expenditure per student among districts, at the state (or province) level, as well as at the federal level. Of course, some additional resources should be allocated to students with special needs, to compensate for disabilities or social disadvantages. But it is only when considering education at the college level and higher that something like a meritocratic implementation of the principle of fair equality of opportunity is useful (and appropriate) for making decisions about the allocation of relatively scarce educational goods.[37] Behind Rawls' theory of justice is a concern to take into account the interests of all members of society. This concern supports the idea that we should ensure that children make the most out of their school years. This is especially true for those children who are not going to pursue a higher education.

Let us now turn briefly to consider the second principle of justice. There are a variety of ways in which one could try to enlist this two-part principle in support of certain forms of distribution of educational goods. Let us begin with the requirements of fair equality of opportunity. The idea that those with similar talents and motivation should have similar life prospects might suggest trying to develop mechanisms to separate children into groups with similar levels of talent and motivation, and then providing each group with an education that 'fits' their level of talent and motivation. But this is the wrong way of implementing the principle. What we normally take as the sort of talent relevant to fair equality of opportunity is in fact 'cultivated talent.' We cannot reliably predict, based on early performance in school, how well children will do in the future, and we should not treat students differently based on unreliable predictions. Moreover, the kinds of talents that children will develop depend to a great extent on educational decisions.[38] As a result, it seems much more plausible to aim for a high level of educational achievement for all children, and to use more selective mechanisms for allocating educational resources only after the age of eighteen. Even if schools differ in what they can offer to children and adolescents, it should not be the case that a child's future position in the labor market is decided very early in life, largely on the basis of family background.

As regards the difference principle, educational policies may contribute to its satisfaction in a number of ways, working with other social policies.

First, they can help develop the capacities and skills of children so that they are capable of making an independent income as adults, whether as employees or as self-employed workers. Having access to economic resources, in turn, is part of what the maximization of the worth of liberty requires. Second, the working of the educational system as a whole may lead to the development of talents and skills that serve to benefit everyone in society, especially the worst off. Of course, this will not happen automatically, no matter how much talent and skill is developed. Rather, there would have to be a number of additional social policies, such as a national health care system, that would help ensure that professional services and other social benefits resulting from the cultivated talents are available to all members of society.

The important point to stress is that for the family to be a just social institution, other parts of the basic structure must work to compensate for those effects of families that tend to deviate from the requirements of social justice. It is plausible that many of these tendencies are unavoidable, and cannot be completely overcome.

5 Reasonable Citizens

Which Institutions Teach the Principles of Justice?

The ideal of a just society entails the existence of certain institutions—those that make up the basic structure of society—that guarantee basic rights and liberties, equality of opportunity, and access to material resources. Such an ideal also presupposes a certain account of reasonable citizens. In particular, reasonable citizens will have a set of moral capacities and dispositions, and will voluntarily support just institutions. This last point is related to the following important consideration in favor of a normative theory of justice: that it be stable. That is, such a theory must be capable of generating its own support over time. This means that it has to be possible for its citizens who live under just institutions to develop a reasonable moral psychology and to come to endorse the principles of justice, integrating them into their personal conceptions of the good life. When Rawls turns to consider the question of how a widespread and deep moral consensus on the principles of justice might be generated in *actual* societies—a question which is closely related to the issue of how such consensus could be maintained over time—he does not pay much attention to the potential contribution of schools to the production of reasonable citizens. This neglect can be explained, in part, by his confidence that the functioning of just institutions will 'spontaneously' generate, in citizens who live under them, the necessary support for principles of justice, and will encourage the development and exercise of the virtues characteristic of reasonable citizens. While the basic structure includes many institutions that might contribute to this outcome, Rawls relies primarily on the effects of the functioning of its political and judicial institutions. He thinks that these institutions in particular have an educational role in a wide sense. In his own words

> Those who grow up in such a society will in good part form their conception of themselves as citizens from the public political culture and from the conceptions of person and society implicit in it. They will see themselves as having certain basic rights and liberties, freedoms they can not only claim for themselves but freedoms they must also respect

in others. Doing this belongs to their conception of themselves as sharing the status of equal citizenship ...

Citizens acquire an understanding of the public political culture and its traditions of interpreting basic constitutional values. They do so by attending to how these values are interpreted by judges in important constitutional cases and reaffirmed by political parties. If disputed judicial decisions—there are bound to be such—call forth deliberative political discussion in the course of which their merits are reasonably debated in terms of constitutional principles, then even these disputed decisions, by drawing citizens into public debate, may serve a vital educational role.[1]

In these passages Rawls asserts that certain ideas implicit in the public culture will come to be understood and accepted by those who live in just democratic societies whose basic institutions embody them. Among these ideas might be, for example, the idea of citizens as free and equal and the idea of society as a fair system of cooperation. Now, it is undeniable that political and judicial institutions have some educational effects. After all, they encourage certain behaviors and discourage others. But Rawls' remarks suggest that he thinks that the operation of these institutions by themselves can do a great deal to generate support for the political values of justice as fairness. He also thinks that democratic procedures and even judicial disputes contribute to this educational task. These claims might well be plausible if one is imaging the workings of an ideal society, in which the major social institutions satisfy the principles of justice and individual behavior also supports just institutional functioning. But they are much less persuasive if they are meant to apply to real societies in which one cannot expect anything close to full compliance with the principles of justice. If we translate his claims from the ideal context to the non-ideal, Rawls' remarks become a misleading idealization. This is because they take a highly selective view of the attitudes and dispositions that institutional functioning encourages in citizens. *Actual* social, political, and economic institutions transmit all sorts of messages: messages that are often in conflict. Nor do these institutions always promote and reward just behavior. For example, it is true that there are aspects of the judicial system that endorse and communicate the normative ideal that all citizens are equal under the law. But as the judicial system actually functions, those who are rich receive, on average, more respectful treatment and less severe punishments. This can easily be taken to communicate the message that wealth entitles a citizen to a different, gentler sort of treatment. Rawls' account of the development of the sense of justice is premised on the idea that people who grow up under just social institutions will perceive that these institutions benefit them, and that this perception will, in turn, generate the desire to support just institutions. It is true that in real societies all citizens benefit at least to some degree from schemes of social cooperation and from the rule of law. But different groups of citizens also suffer different sorts of injustices, some more severe and some less. My point is that nothing guarantees that acquaintance with existing institutions will even make citizens aware of, much less ensure that they endorse, the *best ideals* that these institutions imperfectly embody. Even if we accept that in an ideally just society the functioning of these institutions is sufficient to (unintentionally) educate citizens in the core values of justice as fairness, this 'invisible hand' is not a mechanism that is available to those who are attempting to build societies that are closer to Rawls' model in the first place. Some other mechanism must be sought.

One might of course acknowledge that the functioning of political and judicial institutions alone is not enough to produce an understanding of and support for the best ideals such institutions embody, but then go on to suggest that there are other social institutions that could be trusted to perform this task. In particular, one might claim that the stability of a just society does not require state-regulated education for citizenship, as long as other social institutions—families, unions, the market, civil associations—have the sort of educational effects required to encourage the cultivation of reasonability. If everything worked according to this best case scenario, then there would be no pressing need for the state to regulate public and private schools in order to ensure that the central dispositions of reasonability were taught to each new generation. In this sense, schools' minimal contribution to social justice might be appropriate for Rawls' ideal well-ordered society. But the essential worry about idealization remains, even if we widen the scope of the relevant institutions: in existing liberal democratic societies, it is highly unlikely that these institutions will all fortuitously converge in the right direction and support the dispositions characteristic of reasonable citizens who have an effective sense of justice.[2]

Will Kymlicka has persuasively argued that schools are in a privileged position to teach the central dispositions that support the principles of justice, dispositions that Rawls calls "political virtues."[3] Kymlicka agrees that other social institutions cannot be relied upon to transmit these core political virtues. Briefly, his own argument for this conclusion runs as follows. Although families play a basic role in the education and moral development of children, not all families prepare children to interact with other citizens on the basis of reciprocity and mutual respect. This is because some families inculcate sexist, racist, classist, or intolerant attitudes in their children. So-called 'associations of civil society'—such as churches, clubs, political groups, and neighborhood groups—do, sometimes, encourage the development of skills, interests, and dispositions that support trust, cooperation, and participation in public affairs among citizens. But there are also associations that one might call, following Simone Chambers and Jeffrey Kopstein, instances of "bad civil society."[4] These are groups that function with norms of cooperation and trust among their members, but encourage hatred, intolerance, and distrust of non-members. Kymlicka raises similar concerns about the market, which some claim encourages traits such as responsibility, self-reliance, independence, and even tolerance and civility (because these attitudes would be good for business). As Kymlicka points out, the market may also be a school for greed and economic irresponsibility, and it may provide incentives for businesses to discriminate in their hiring practices or in their treatment of clients (for example, when there is a prejudiced majority that prefers not to interact with members of certain minority groups). Similarly, some suggest that the practice of political participation itself will promote public spiritedness, responsibility, and tolerance. But again nothing guarantees that political participation will not be motivated by factional interests, or by prejudices against minorities. Although all these social institutions will inevitably teach *some* lessons about how to interact with others on fair terms, they will not always, or even reliably, teach the *right* ones. In contrast, schools are in a much better position to fulfill the task of teaching the political virtues. One reason for this is that schools are charged with a significant portion of children's education. Another reason is that what takes place in schools can be planned and publicly monitored in ways that are not feasible for other institutions, at least not without excessive levels of intrusion.

It is to be expected that some will object to Kymlicka's argument for assigning schools a central role in the teaching of reasonability, expressing worries that allowing this teaching will open the door to state indoctrination and the brainwashing of children. But such concerns are exaggerated when we are considering liberal democratic societies, even if they may be plausible in other kinds of societies. In liberal democracies there are multiple levels of public regulation and control of the functioning of schools, and these provide something like 'checks and balances.' Moreover, there are institutionalized means for parents and teachers to raise complaints and press for changes. These considerations support the case for state regulation of children's education, with the aim of ensuring that children are taught to have dispositions to cooperate with others on fair terms. This is one important way in which schools can contribute to the achievement of a just society in which the rights and liberties of citizens are respected. Of course, there are other considerations—even more directly grounded in the requirements of justice—that should play a role when making public decisions about educational policy, such as securing equality of opportunity and preparing children to participate effectively in the economy. But these are not our present concern.

Schools are perhaps the obvious candidate to play the 'stability-enhancing' role described earlier. But Rawls seems very reluctant to assign any significant role to them. Why is this? Together with his trust in some sort of invisible hand to generate a deep moral consensus on the right kind of political values, Rawls' hesitation to put any emphasis on schools' contribution to social justice may also be explained by his concerns about the limits of justifiable public policy. As we have seen, Rawls advocates a method of political justification for the principles of justice that avoids reliance on comprehensive views about the good, and that appeals instead to ideals that are widely shared. In this connection, Rawls briefly discusses the civic aims of the education of children as an example of the difference between political liberalism on the one hand, and partially comprehensive liberal theories on the other. According to Rawls, any justification of the goals of an educational system for children should avoid appeal to comprehensive liberal ideals of the good life such as personal autonomy or individuality. The reason for this restriction on justification is that not all reasonable citizens can be expected to endorse these ideals.[5] As against such perfectionistic forms of justification, Rawls claims that guidelines for the education of children can be justified politically, by taking into account their role as future citizens. This implies that schools should aim at creating good citizens who will support the creation and maintenance of just social institutions. Because Rawls tries to mark a contrast between the scope and generality of the political liberalism he advocates and the scope and generality of comprehensive liberal theories, he describes the education that derives from political liberalism in (apparently) minimalist terms. Partly this is because he wants to emphasize that certain educational goals cannot be justified, and partly it is because he is only mentioning those specific goals that best serve to illustrate the contrast he is concerned with making. But as I will argue in the final sections of this chapter, the education that supports social transformation in the direction of social justice is, unavoidably, quite robust. However, before discussing this issue, it is necessary to be clearer on what, as per Rawls, is the nature of political justification.

Political Justification of Policy

Rawls claims that the only adequate strategy for the justification of policy concerning matters of basic justice in pluralist societies is one that is restricted to political arguments: arguments that avoid appeal to comprehensive doctrines that might not be shared by all reasonable citizens. Some authors have phrased this requirement in terms of the claim that the state should be *neutral* with regard to its citizens' conceptions of the good. But there are many interpretations of neutrality, so it is worth examining the particular sort of neutrality that Rawls' strategy supports. To begin with, one might understand neutrality in terms of *neutrality of consequences or effects*. On this understanding, one might say that the state should aim to promote (or restrict) all citizens' conceptions of the good to the same degree. But as many have pointed out, this type of neutrality is not a practicable ideal. We can dismiss it simply by pointing out that public policies and laws will unavoidably have a differential impact on citizens' opportunities to pursue their own conceptions of the good, favoring some conceptions and limiting others. Beyond this, and as Will Kymlicka has argued, Rawls' own theory is in fact incompatible with neutrality of consequences, because the principles of justice have nonneutral effects on people's capacity to pursue their plans of life. For instance, even a maximally fair distribution of primary goods will affect the plans of life of different people in different ways, because not all plans have the same costs.[6]

Opposed to the idea of neutrality of consequences is *neutrality of justification*. Some authors have defended the idea of *procedural justificatory neutrality*, which involves using a decision-making procedure that can be justified without appealing to any moral values, or at least only by appealing to allegedly neutral values such as impartiality, consistency in the application of principles, or equality of opportunity to present demands.[7] One might well be skeptical about such an approach, doubting the possibility of justifications that appeal to no hidden moral values or doubting the coherence of the very idea of neutral values. But there is no need to settle these matters here. Rawls denies that his theory can be regarded as procedurally neutral, since it is based on the substantive ideals of free and equal citizenship, and of society as a fair system of cooperation. These ideals already, by themselves, rule out the permissibility of some comprehensive doctrines, such as racist doctrines that deny equal status to all citizens, or doctrines that incorporate a view of society as organized for the benefit of the stronger, and that reject the idea that all members should benefit, at least to a certain degree, from social cooperation. Although Rawls' political theory of justice attempts to uncover a public basis of justification for social arrangements that all reasonable citizens can share, the common framework it provides is not procedurally neutral: it is based, at its deepest level, on certain moral values implicit in the public culture of democratic societies.

Procedural justificatory neutrality is, however, not the only type of justificatory neutrality. Rawls mentions another type, claiming that his theory incorporates a view of justificatory neutrality that he describes as *neutrality of aims*. To claim that the state should be neutral in this way involves two claims: (a) that one of the state's aims should be to secure equality of opportunity to pursue any conception of the good that is consistent with the requirements of justice; (b) that no state action should have, as its goal, the favoring of any doctrine in particular, again, among those consistent with the requirements of justice.[8] It isn't entirely clear why (a) and (b) should be considered to express a form of neutrality, except in the sense that there is no intent to take sides on the issue of which conceptions of the good are true or valuable, provided they are consistent with the principles of justice.

However, Rawls also makes use of another kind of justificatory neutrality, that we can call *restrictive justificatory neutrality*, although he does not call it by that name, or indeed refer to it as a form of neutrality. Restrictive justificatory neutrality has its source in Rawls' idea that the justification of policies—at least those that touch on basic issues of justice— should be restricted to what he calls 'public reasons.'[9] These are reasons that all reasonable citizens could find acceptable. To find a reason acceptable of course does not mean that one must find it to be definitive. It only means that one finds it to be of obvious relevance to deciding the issue on which it has a bearing. By making use of the idea of public reasons as he does, Rawls is in fact endorsing a form of justificatory neutrality. This form of justificatory neutrality does not depend on the idea that all considerations of the good should be excluded from the process of political decision making. Rather, it is the idea that the state should abstain from basing its decisions on grounds that could be reasonably rejected by some citizens. That is, restrictive justificatory neutrality is the idea that the state should base its decisions on public reasons. The fact that reasons are appealed to in justifying policies of course means that some values will be relevant. But in fact, not only is it undesirable, it is actually impossible to exclude all values from the process of justification of public policies. Political arguments in favor of particular policies appeal to certain goods or benefits they will provide, or to certain evils that they will reduce or prevent, or to normative principles and ideals that should be respected.[10] Restrictive justificatory neutrality is a more useful notion than neutrality of aims because the specific aims of laws and public policies are not easily discernible unless we already know the justifications that are offered for them. Moreover, what makes policies with neutral aims attractive is precisely the fact that they can be justified to people who adhere to different comprehensive doctrines. Although restrictive justificatory neutrality rules out certain kinds of considerations as acceptable reasons to support public policies, not all the considerations that pass the test of neutrality—not all public reasons—will have the same weight. And, perhaps unfortunately, restrictive justificatory neutrality does not tell us exactly how to strike a fair balance among acceptable considerations.[11] The principles of justice are meant to provide some background considerations that serve as a guide for laws and policy. But more particularized reasoning and relevant empirical information—and even some trial and error—are also required if we are to come up with fair and sensible policies.

The requirement of neutrality of the state has received a variety of criticisms, some of which are encouraged by the highly misleading connotations of the term. Many of the critics of neutrality simply understand neutrality as neutrality as regards values in general, or as neutrality of consequences, and declare it to be an untenable ideal. This does nothing to undermine the appeal of Rawls' political theory of justice because he does not rely on any such interpretation of neutrality. But there have also been more radical objections that do not depend so crucially on a misreading of Rawls. From a communitarian neo-Aristotelian perspective, Alasdair MacIntyre has criticized the "privatization of the good" involved in centering public debate on a set of principles and procedures, while leaving the task of developing, defending, and pursuing particular conceptions of the good to the private sphere.[12] MacIntyre argues that one cannot invoke shared rules or principles independently of a shared conception of the human good. This conception of the human good, in turn, must be embodied in the practices of particular communities such as families, schools, hospitals, churches, or neighbor-hoods. To a certain extent, MacIntyre is right when he points out the diffi-culty or impossibility of justifying social policies without using some notion of the good. However, he wrongly holds that in order to play this justifica-tory role moral rules or principles have to be identified and characterized as part of the specification of some particular complete and holistic view about the human good, that is, as part of a comprehensive doctrine. In a pluralistic society, the implications of such a position lead to a false dilemma, sug-gesting that we must either homogenize society by imposing a complete and holistic view of the good, or renounce all attempts to transmit a shared set of norms and procedures. It is true that if we acknowledge the fact of plur-alism and the importance of public justifiability, we cannot in consistency appeal to comprehensive ideals of the human good as the basis of public policy. However, accepting the requirements of restrictive justificatory neu-trality still allows us to construct thinner notions of the good, by appealing to values that are shared (or not rejected) by the adherents of different comprehensive doctrines. The requirements of neutrality do not eliminate the possibility of an appeal to common values, such as those ideals implicit in the public culture. They are also compatible with appeals to shared practices and procedures that are acceptable for reasonable citizens who hold different comprehensive doctrines. The strategy of political justification avoids MacIntyre's false dilemma, because it acknowledges both the exis-tence of disagreements about comprehensive views about the good, and the need to find principles of justice and procedures that can regulate the inter-actions of citizens in a fair way.[13]

Educating Reasonable Citizens

We have already seen that, according to Rawls, children will somehow need to be educated so that they acquire the dispositions characteristic of rea-sonable citizens. Otherwise we have no reason to expect a society organized around his principles to be stable. But Rawls needs to show that the state can require the provision of such an education by schools—public or pri-vate—while still satisfying the requirements of restrictive justificatory neu-trality. This is one of the reasons why he contrasts the educational implications of a political liberal theory with those of comprehensive liberal theories. In making this contrast he stresses that, according to his political theory of justice, schools should not try to encourage the development of autonomy or individuality in children. Rather, they will do much less:

> It will ask that children's education include such things as knowledge of their constitutional and civil rights, so that, for example, they know that liberty of conscience exists in their society and that apostasy is not a legal crime, all this to ensure that their continued religious member-ship when they come of age is not based simply on ignorance of their

basic rights or fear of punishment for offenses that are only considered offenses within their religious sect. Their education should also prepare them to be fully cooperating members of society and enable them to be self-supporting; it should also encourage the political virtues so that they want to honor the fair terms of social cooperation in their relations with the rest of society.[14]

Later he adds that:

The state's concern with their education lies in their role as future citizens, and so in such essential things as their acquiring the capacity to understand the public culture and to participate in its institutions, in their being economically independent and self-supporting members of society over a complete life, and in their developing the political virtues, all this from within a political point of view.[15]

Unfortunately for Rawls, these claims about the education of future citizens do not serve to mark a particularly sharp contrast between his political theory of justice as fairness and more comprehensive liberal theories. The problem for Rawls' argument is that even if the educational goals he endorses do not appeal to comprehensive ideals about how people should live their lives, they still include the encouragement of the political virtues. And the complex set of dispositions that are characteristic of reasonable citizens who exercise the political virtues can only be instilled by an education that will have significant effects on their character.[16] Rawls himself admits that the kind of education he advocates may have an influence on the conceptions of the good of students, favoring some and weakening others. When the different interpretations of the requirement of neutrality were presented earlier, one thing that was pointed out was the futility of aspiring to a neutrality of effects for any kind of public policy. In fact, Rawls concedes that one might object to his proposal by claiming that teaching a political conception of justice would be equivalent, in practice if not in intention, to teaching a particular comprehensive liberal view. Apparently Rawls believes that the only possible answer to this objection consists in pointing out the differences in scope and generality between his theory and comprehensive liberal ones. But this is not a good defense. It is true that the educational requirements of Rawls' theory are more limited than those of liberal comprehensive theories, in the very restricted sense that the former focus on an education for citizenship, and avoid discussing the issue of how people should live their lives in general. As regards the scope of different political and comprehensive liberal theories, there may be some differences in their educational application, but they are not as clear cut as Rawls claims. As we have seen, Rawls' account of education for citizenship is not as minimal as it might initially seem, since it includes the cultivation of political virtues that depend on the development of the capacity for reasonability. And, I will argue further later, this capacity cannot be culti-vated without educational practices that explore the diversity of views about the good life. These 'exploratory' practices are of course similar in impor-tant respects to those advocated by comprehensive liberals. In the second place, as Amy Gutmann and Eamonn Callan have independently shown, the educational implications of different comprehensive liberal theories are far from homogeneous, since they depend on the different assumptions and claims that structure the theories.[17] As a consequence, although some comprehensive liberal theories may recommend educational practices that are ruled out by Rawls' political approach, other comprehensive liber-alisms may overlap very significantly with Rawls' in their educational recommendations.[18]

I think we should conclude, therefore, that Rawls' own attempts to dis-tinguish his view from more comprehensive liberalisms by pointing to dif-ferences in educational policy fail. But I also think that Rawls has more effective resources for answering the worry that his view really cannot be distinguished from these other forms of liberalism. True, his view may have very similar educational implications to those of some comprehensive liber-alisms. But it simply does not follow from the fact that two different the-ories overlap in their educational policies, that the theories are equivalent, even as regards education.[19] The main difference between the educational approach supported by justice as fairness and other liberal views is not to be found in their content, but in the sorts of arguments employed to justify them. A theory that aims to be political (in Rawls' technical use of the term) would always limit itself to arguments that are acceptable to all reasonable citizens. This gives a political theory a theoretical advantage in justifying the policies it advocates. Moreover, a political theory of justice also has prac-tical advantages. The very same policy, when defended by political argu-ments, may have wider appeal and gain more stable support than when defended using contentious evaluative concepts. Finally, when one's educa-tional policy is based on a comprehensive doctrine that happens to be a liberal one, there is no guarantee that future shifts in the popularity of that doctrine will allow the same sort of educational policy to persist. But if that policy is defended in political terms, such shifts will not have as great a practical impact. In conclusion, Rawls' account of education for citizenship is not minimal, but it is still political.

Once we free ourselves from the idea that a Rawlsian civic education must be minimal, it will be easier to see the sorts of problems that it must address, and to develop strategies for addressing them. One set of problems have their source in the diversity of comprehensive moral, religious, and philosophical doctrines associated with the conceptions of the good life endorsed by adult citizens.[20] This diversity presents schools with significant challenges. In non-ideal contexts, we cannot assume that all adult citizens are reasonable or that other social, political, and economic institutions are likely to generate massive support for the principles of justice. The task of schools in generating and reproducing commitment to the principles of justice in younger generations is therefore both more difficult and more urgent. One central goal of schools in non-ideal contexts is to foster the wide acceptance of common norms, principles, and procedures that provide a certain coherence and viability to social life, and that allow the different members of society to get along together in a respectful democratic way. And given the plurality of comprehensive doctrines that citizens endorse, it is also necessary to encourage attitudes of understanding, mental openness, and tolerance when confronted with views of the good life that are different from one's own. As we have seen, these attitudes are expressions of the capacity for reasonability, which includes the disposition to cooperate with others on reciprocal terms and to accept the burdens of judgment.

The distinction between public principles on the one hand and comprehensive doctrines on the other, might lead one to think that the education of citizens should only focus on the former, aiming to bring students to appreciate and accept certain political principles, norms, and procedures. With regard to comprehensive doctrines and other less-structured general views of the good, it might be tempting to adopt what Kenneth Strike calls "liberal silence."[21] As Strike vividly describes it:

> Liberal silence occurs when schools try to avoid moral questions, making minimal efforts to teach only the common morality. In schools where liberal silence prevails, the voices of particular moral communities are silenced because they are not shared. We fear our differences and the controversy they invite, so we create schools that extol mutual respect and tolerance but resist any real exploration of competing moral visions.[22]

One reason to adopt the strategy of liberal silence might be that schools would thereby avoid undue influence on the beliefs and values of students when it comes to their developing a conception of the good. This sort of reasoning assumes that education in pluralist democratic societies should remain silent on controversial issues, and that explicitly avoiding an issue is the most appropriate way to allow students to develop their own convictions. Another reason why this strategy may tempt some policy-makers is their belief that being silent about controversial issues is a good way to avoid conflicts.[23] But is liberal silence in schools really an implication of Rawls' justice as fairness? As we have seen, acknowledging the plurality of conceptions of the good that reasonable citizens may endorse imposes certain requirements on the state. The first of these requirements is that the state cannot require schools to impose a particular conception of the good. Call this the negative requirement. But a second requirement is that schools should encourage the active acceptance of public norms, principles, and procedures, together with dispositions for tolerance and mutual understanding, as well as other political virtues. Call this the positive requirement. Although adopting a policy of liberal silence seems compatible with the negative requirement, it is clearly deficient as regards the positive requirement. Remaining silent about the existence of controversies about the good does not contribute to the promotion of political virtues, for these virtues require a developed capacity for reasonability. Unfortunately, an education that attempts to satisfy the second requirement will almost certainly transgress the first one to some extent. This is because teaching tolerance and other political virtues inevitably involves introducing liberal notions into schemes of thought that are not necessarily open to them, and as a consequence these less liberal schemes of thought will be cast into some doubt. But unless the positive requirement receives no weight at all, liberal silence cannot be endorsed by a Rawlsian.

In designing an educational proposal that will satisfy the requirements of public justifiability and that strives both to encourage reasonability and to promote an understanding of political principles, norms, and procedures, one must consider whether or not it should deal explicitly with the fact of reasonable disagreement among citizens who hold different conceptions of the good. That is, one must ask whether it should encourage the exploration and discussion of a variety of conceptions of the good, or whether it should, to the contrary, remain silent about them and their unavoidable disagreements. Rawls is very cautious in his brief references to the education of future citizens and tries to reduce its requirements to a minimum. Because of this, one might infer that he does favor a policy of liberal silence. However, the unity and stability of a society that aspires to satisfy the principles of justice cannot be sustained without the reflective acceptance of the principles by each new generation. Callan has persuasively argued that the logic of the Rawlsian argument leads to the inclusion, in citizenship education, of a certain sort of exploration of conceptions of the good. A central claim in Callan's argument is that the development of capacities that make for reasonability is not possible without a real awareness of the scope of diversity that exists in society. Reasonable citizens have, for example, the capacity for reciprocity, which involves, among other things, being capable of making proposals that one considers fair, and being willing to listen and discuss the proposals of others.[24] One cannot do this unless one really understands the points of view of others, and accepts the possibility of reasonable disagreements between people with different comprehensive views. Put in terms of a technical notion that we discussed in chapter 3, reasonable citizens will accept the burdens of judgment. Accepting these "burdens" will lead reasonable citizens to accept, in turn, certain restrictions on the sorts of arguments they can offer in political discussion. That is, it will lead them to try to express their proposals in terms of public reasons. Callan has also argued that, along with the development of the disposition to cooperate with others and to accept the burdens of judgment, it is necessary for civic education to cultivate the intellectual capacity to figure out which sources of conflict depend on the burdens of judgment and which are due to lack of reasonability (such as logical mistakes or undue egoism or factionalism).[25] These considerations support the idea that the education of citizens will need to include an examination of the diversity of views about the good life and of the kinds of controversies this diversity tends to generate. Designing an education for citizenship that satisfies the demands of public justifiability does not require giving up the idea of cultivating reasonability. And if it is designed with the ideal of reasonable citizens in mind, such education cannot be as minimal as Rawls indicates.

Another way in which Rawls has substantial implications for educational policy has to do with the distinction between political norms and the norms internal to comprehensive doctrines. In this connection, Terrence McLaughlin has proposed that, when one teaches students about political norms, principles, and procedures, their character and scope must be made clear.[26] That is, it is important to make clear that those principles and procedures cover only one aspect of the moral life and not the whole of it. This feature of political principles is part of what allows us to offer a restricted public justification for them. Moreover, when certain ways of life or conceptions of the good are discussed, one thing that should be explained is that even though they must be accepted or tolerated in the public realm, that does not always make them completely acceptable from the point of view of other conceptions of the good. In other words, when teaching moral issues we should distinguish between: (a) what is completely acceptable from a political perspective and any comprehensive doctrine held by reasonable citizens (for example, the validity of fundamental human rights); and (b) what is acceptable from the political perspective, but it is not completely acceptable for some reasonable comprehensive view (for example, the moral permissibility of intercourse among consenting adults who are not married). At the same time that one explains the difference between political principles, procedures, and norms on the one hand, and moral perspectives derived from comprehensive doctrines on the other, one could also try to offer political justifications for the former principles and procedures, as well as to demonstrate their compatibility with reasonable comprehensive doctrines.[27] Finally, schools should try to cultivate the interpretive capacities of children to help them understand a variety of comprehensive doctrines that are different from their own. These educational tasks seem essential to the formation of reasonable citizens who acknowledge the existence of reasonable disagreements about the good, and still agree on a framework of common principles, norms, and procedures of public policy.

The Objection from Perfectionism

If the preceding recommendations are correct, it seems that Rawls has described the educational implications of his theory in misleading terms. However that might be, our more demanding reading of the educational implications of Rawls's theory gives rise to the following objection: the exploration of a wide variety of moral perspectives in schools may erode the basis of certain students' acceptance of creeds and ways of life, especially when these were transmitted by their families in a dogmatic way that denied the existence of reasonable alternatives. This "erosion effect" may seem objectionable because it implies that the development of the capacities and virtues necessary for sustaining a just society tends to promote the adoption of a critical attitude towards conceptions of the good and the comprehensive doctrines that sustain them. In other words, one may object that the robust form of Rawlsian civic education favors the exercise of personal autonomy, which turns out to be the hidden core value that grounds it. Call this the objection from perfectionism.

The objection from perfectionism assumes that autonomy lies at the heart of some particular conception of the good that would be privileged in an unjustifiable way by a Rawlsian education for citizenship. Against this assumption, education for reasonable citizenship leaves indeterminate many issues that are central to any personal view of what a good life is, and does not aim to challenge students' reasonable convictions. Because of this, the education of citizens will not be incompatible with the education that reasonable parents want to give their children. The arguments I have presented start from the premise that it is necessary to teach political virtues such as tolerance and mutual understanding, the possession of which by most citizens is required if society's basic institutions are to make room for the pursuit of a variety of plans of life. If the teaching of these virtues erodes the basis for belief in dogmatic or intolerant views that deny the rights of others to develop their plans of life, this is not something to be criticized but is rather something in favor of the proposal.

The objection from perfectionism might well have some bite against certain non-political (that is, comprehensive) liberal approaches. But, when it comes to dealing with the problem of designing educational policies in pluralistic societies, the theoretical framework of justice as fairness is better than non-political approaches precisely because it does *not* presuppose the moral superiority of conceptions of the good that incorporate the exercise of personal autonomy. Like any liberal proposal, justice as fairness is concerned with setting up a framework of institutions that allows citizens to develop and pursue their own conceptions of the good. In this sense, it defends the political autonomy of citizens: their authority to live their lives as they choose. But this approach is justified in terms of public reasons, and not in terms of the assertion of the intrinsic value of an autonomous life. Liberal proposals that are built on the intrinsic value of autonomy tend not to be acceptable to those who profess non-autonomist but reasonable conceptions of the good. This is precisely the reason that such proposals fall prey to the objection from perfectionism. A perfectionist view holds, in general terms, that the design of public policy and the distribution of resources and opportunities in a society ought to be decided on the basis of differential judgments about the relative values of different conceptions of the good. Because of this, perfectionist policies are liable to be inconsistent with respect for the capacity of citizens to make their own decisions with regard to which conception of the good they will pursue. But, the objection holds, public policies should be capable of justification without appealing to moral considerations that adherents to one or another conception of the good could reasonably reject. Now, as we have seen, the idea of public reason that is so central to Rawls' view is not that all substantive moral values should be excluded from the process of public justification. Rather, it is that we should exclude considerations that adherents to reasonable comprehensive doctrines could have grounds to reject. So a political liberalism is consonant with the rationale behind the objection from perfectionism, when that objection is directed at non-political liberal views.

Despite the foregoing arguments, one might still try to hold that Rawls' proposal does not avoid perfectionism, since it recommends the teaching of political virtues. Recommending the teaching of virtue, the objection goes, involves an implicit commitment to ideals of human excellence and human flourishing that not all reasonable citizens endorse. Rawls does not say much about the political virtues, but he describes them as those traits of character of reasonable citizens that help to support the two principles of justice. In my view, one can understand these virtues in general terms as complex dispositions of perception, emotion, judgment, and behavior that are essential to the maintenance of fair social cooperation. What makes this account of virtue a political account is that the value of such traits is explained in terms of their contribution to the fulfillment of political principles of justice, instead of by appeal to comprehensive doctrines. To give a couple of examples, one virtue that can be defended in political terms is toleration, and another is civility.[28] It is easy to show that the education of citizens should include among its justified tasks the teaching of these kinds of virtues. Cultivating these traits in schools can be justified politically without any need to take sides on the question of what constitutes human flourishing or human excellence: one can argue that citizens' possessing these virtues is necessary for a society to satisfy the principles of justice. The following example by Will Kymlicka may be useful to illustrate this point. Let us assume that in a particular society the laws prohibit racial discrimination, but that businesses nevertheless persist in discriminating when they select employees or when they decide on promotions. Suppose also that when real estate companies offer properties they restrict some areas on the basis of racial or ethnic criteria. Even if there are laws against discrimination and the state itself does not discriminate, the persistence of such practices is an obstacle to social justice. For social justice requires that all citizens be treated as equals, and that there be fair equality of opportunity to access to jobs and positions of authority.[29] The point is that such discriminatory practices cannot be ended by law alone, even when the law carries the threat of legal sanction. One reason for this is that the law may be difficult to implement in many cases. As a result, a certain level of virtue among citizens must supplement the law for society to be fully just.

As the preceding example reminds us, there are many sources of injustice in non-ideal societies. This fact extends the implications of Rawls' theory for education for citizenship. Even in ideal contexts, the exercise of political virtues requires a complex set of capacities for reasoning and feeling that are necessary to respond in an adequate manner to the challenges of social interaction in contexts of pluralism and diversity. But in imperfect societies, citizens also need to be able to figure out what justice requires when they are faced with norms and established practices that are not always fair, and they also need to come up with plausible strategies for social transformation. These may include protests, lawsuits, civil disobedience, and other measures. As a consequence, the task of encouraging the political virtues in non-ideal contexts may become quite demanding. Education for citizenship must satisfy the requirements of public justifiability, but the teaching of political virtues of reasonable citizens will also have transformative goals, at least while societies continue to fail to live up to the ideals of freedom and equality that their constitutional order proclaims.

6   Free and Equal Citizens

The Basic Liberties and their Worth

One of the central elements of Rawls' argument in support of the two principles of justice is the intuitive normative ideal of citizens as free and equal.[1] Rawls takes this ideal to play an important role in explaining and justifying the design of the original position. He also holds that the ideal is implicit in the public culture of contemporary democratic societies, and that it is present in the design and functioning of their political and legal institutions. For these reasons he claims that the ideal can be regarded as widely shared. Perhaps this is true. Still, taken in isolation, the claim that citizens are to be treated as free and equal is indeterminate, and has virtually no clear implications for policy. In order to remedy this, the two principles of justice, together with the stipulation that citizens have basic interests in developing their moral capacities and in pursuing their conceptions of the good life, are meant to provide a more precise and useful interpretation of what is involved in treating citizens as free and equal. The first principle of justice requires that society secure a scheme of equal basic rights and liberties for all its citizens. The second principle asserts that social and economic inequalities are permissible only when the following two conditions are met: that there is fair equality of opportunity to access desirable social positions, and that any such inequalities work to the benefit of everyone, particularly the least advantaged members of society. However, it is by no means obvious that satisfying Rawls' two principles of justice is the most appropriate or plausible way to uphold the status of citizens as free and equal—or so argue some of Rawls' critics. In relation to this debate, the present chapter has three aims. The first is to examine Rawls' account of the type of freedom that a just society must guarantee equally to its citizens. I will argue that those who think of Rawls as a theorist of freedom as non-interference are mistaken, because the notion of liberty at work in the first principle of justice resembles, in important respects, a particular notion of freedom as non-domination that Philip Pettit has defended as central to the republican tradition. Second, I will consider the extent to which Rawls' principles of justice successfully protect the freedom as non-domination of all citizens so as to treat them effectively as free and equal. Finally, I will briefly discuss the contributions that schools might make to support the ideal of citizens as free and equal. In discussing these contributions, it will be important to keep in mind that Rawls' political approach to the justification of policies implicitly involves a number of restrictions on the form such support can take.

Although Rawls sometimes refers to liberty in general terms, it is clear from his discussion of the notion of liberty that he has in mind a set of specific liberties that should be granted to the citizens of a just society. As we saw in chapter 2, when the principles of justice were first introduced, Rawls specifies the basic rights and liberties of citizens by means of a short list:[2]

1. Liberty of conscience and freedom of thought.
2. Freedom of association.
3. Equal political liberties.
4. Rights and liberties that protect the integrity and freedom of the person.
5. Rights and liberties covered by the rule of law.

As has already been mentioned, this list is largely inspired by the history of struggles for various kinds of liberties: struggles which led to their constitutional protection for all citizens. But the selection of these liberties is also based on Rawls' account of citizens as free and equal, and as having an interest in developing their moral capacities and pursuing reasonable plans of life.

Although there has been some controversy over the question of whether Rawls holds a negative or a positive conception of freedom, he himself explicitly tries to avoid labeling his account of liberty in one way or the other.[3] Following Gerald MacCallum, he claims that we can explain any liberty in terms of three elements: what counts as an agent, what counts as a restriction on freedom, and what activities agents are free to engage in or refrain from.[4] In Rawls' own words:

> The general description of a liberty, then, has the following form: this or that person (or persons) is free (or not free) from this or that constraint (or set of constraints) to do (or not to do) so and so. Associations as well as natural persons may be free or not free, and constraints may range from duties and prohibitions defined by law to the coercive influences arising from public opinion and social pressure. For the most part, I shall discuss liberty in connection with constitutional and legal restrictions. In these cases liberty is a certain structure of institutions, a certain system of public rules defining rights and duties. Set in this background, persons are at liberty to do something when their doing it or not doing it is protected from interference by other persons.[5]

A careful reading of Rawls' list of the basic rights and liberties shows that he takes the class of relevant basic agents to be limited to individual persons and that the liberties that associations may have to act as collective agents turn out to be derivative, and to be dependent on the liberties of individuals.[6] As the earlier paragraph makes explicit, Rawls takes the relevant constraints on liberty to be those defined by law. That is, he excludes as possible infringements on freedom—in the case of the basic liberties—not only the effects of the informal sanctions of public opinion, but also natural obstacles and internal psychological obstacles to action. Finally, the list of basic liberties establishes a range of protections for what are considered the central interests of citizens. That is, the list provides a set of criteria that indicate which types of actions or activities it is most important that the laws protect.

Some neo-republican critics of Rawls—including Jean-Fabien Spitz, Philip Pettit, and Quentin Skinner—read Rawls' claims as an endorsement of a negative conception of freedom; they take Rawls to understand freedom in terms of non-interference. They then go on to argue that this conception of freedom makes the absence of interference an ideal situation of liberty, so that ideal liberty can be enjoyed even (perhaps ideally) in the absence of other people.[7] But while this latter claim might be true of a very simplistic conception of freedom as non-interference, it certainly does not apply to Rawls' developed account of citizens' basic rights and liberties. All of Rawls' basic liberties are liberties of *citizens*, and are granted by political and legal institutions. Some of them—such as freedom of conscience, freedom of association, and political liberties—do not even make sense in the absence of other people. Furthermore, Rawls never says that citizens enjoy these liberties whenever they do not suffer from actual interference. Rather, he says that in order to enjoy them, there must be an adequate system of these liberties, so that citizens are effectively protected against interference (from the actions of individuals, groups, or the state) by political and legal institutions.

A further complication for efforts to put any well-established label on Rawls' conception of liberty is that his theory of justice as fairness recognizes the need for economic resources as a necessary condition on citizens' being able to take advantage of their liberties in pursuing their distinct conceptions of the good life. In Rawls' view, a just society is a society that respects and supports its citizens' development of different conceptions of the good life, and that enables its citizens to pursue these conceptions as they themselves conceive them. This kind of activity is appropriately understood as an exercise of positive freedom, though this should not be understood in a sense that involves a developed conception of personal autonomy. Rather, it amounts to granting citizens the authority and means to decide how to live their lives.[8]

It is true that Rawls does not think that a lack of economic resources—or a lack of knowledge or ability—undermines the claim that citizens have the basic liberties. However, he does claim that such deprivations can affect the "worth" of these liberties. As was mentioned in chapter 2, the worth of a liberty is a measure that depends both on the ability that a citizen has to make use of that liberty, and on the degree to which the exercise of that liberty is useful or essential to the realization of that citizen's plan of life. Because a lack of money, knowledge, or ability can affect the usefulness of a liberty in the effective pursuit of a plan of life (which the theory is concerned to protect), the worth of a liberty will therefore always depend on a citizen's values, inclinations, talents, material resources, and social position. Each citizen will value his or her basic liberties in different ways: some will be very involved in political affairs and give more importance to their political liberties; others may work as journalists, poets, or artists and will make more extensive use of their freedom of expression; members of a third group may devote a significant part of their time and resources to religious observance, and so on. Because the second principle of justice allows certain inequalities in the allotment of desirable social positions and of economic resources, the exercise of basic liberties will turn out to be much easier for some citizens than for others. This might initially seem unfair, but minimal reflection shows that the goal of equalizing the worth of liberty is as difficult as that of equalizing individual well-being. As Rex Martin puts it:

> To assure equal value, we would have to create a homogeneous class of persons—alike, for example, in vocational interests—and place them in similar circumstances. Since Rawls assumes throughout that there will be significant differences among persons in the real social world, it is no part of his program to achieve equality in fact for the actual value of liberties to various persons.[9]

However, this is not to claim that any distribution of the value of the liberties is acceptable for Rawls. Rather, Rawls claims that the difference principle ensures that the worth of the liberties of the worst off members of society will always be greater than it would be if economic resources were distributed more equally.[10]

In an article written in the early seventies, Norman Daniels criticized Rawls' claim that citizens' liberties could be equal while, at the same time, the worth of their liberties was significantly unequal.[11] Because the second principle of justice does not set an absolute limit to the degree of permissible inequality, Daniels pointed out that there is a plausible reading of the theory of justice as fairness that legitimizes very significant inequalities of power, authority, and economic resources among citizens. Daniels then argued that historical experience has shown that even if wealthy and poor citizens have the same formal political liberties, the unequal worth of these liberties will result in wealthier citizens having a systematic advantage in their exercise of political influence. Wealthier citizens are far more capable of influencing the selection of candidates by contributing to political campaigns, and they are more capable of influencing public opinion by controlling the media. Many other similar facts could be cited. As a result, individually unobjectionable instances of the exercise of political liberty—instances that the theory treats as permissible—will have a tendency, taken together over time, to produce structural results such that the interests of the wealthier and more powerful citizens are ultimately over-represented in the democratic processes and resulting laws and policies. This might seem to be a merely empirical argument, but Daniels correctly points out that the likelihood of this tendency challenges the stability of Rawls' ideal model of a just society. It suggests that the theory is not realizable under favorable conditions, or that, even if it were realizable, that support for the principles of justice could not easily be sustained over time as inequalities became more and more pronounced.[12]

In response to Daniels' criticism, Rawls conceded that allowing the worth of all the basic liberties to be unequal brought with it a number of unfortunate foreseeable consequences. He therefore modified the first principle of justice to include a requirement that guaranteed the equal worth of a certain subset of basic liberties. This subset is made up of the specifically *political* liberties. This new requirement, according to Rawls, can be met by restructuring the funding of elections, by subsidizing public debates, and by other measures designed to equalize the opportunities that citizens have to influence the political process.[13] This modification of the first principle of justice may seem to be an *ad hoc* response to Daniels' criticism. But it can also be seen as a principled response to the fact that the political liberties have a competitive aspect. That is, the *relative* quantities of resources that citizens have available, and which they can use to exercise their political liberties, will significantly affect their prospects of influencing the outcome of political processes.[14] It is worth noticing that Rawls seems to think that the other basic liberties are different from the political liberties in this respect. In particular, he thinks that for those citizens who are interested in exercising one of their basic non-political liberties, it is always better simply to secure the highest possible amount of economic resources. That is, in determining whether one economic arrangement is better for them than another with respect to the worth of a given non-political liberty, Rawls seems to think that there is no need to consider the relative economic positions of different people. For example, my interest in exercising my freedom of conscience is necessarily satisfied to a higher degree if I have a greater amount of economic resources (and leisure) available to devote to religious activities, than if I have fewer economic resources (and leisure). And this is true independently of the amount of resources that other people have to pursue similar activities. Thus, Rawls' idea that it is consistent with justice that citizens have equal liberty but unequal worth of liberty presupposes that the interests of citizens in exercising their liberties (excluding the political liberties) will be served in a fair way by the workings of the second principle of justice. This implies that the least advantaged citizens' interest in making use of these basic liberties is better satisfied by the fair equality of opportunity principle taken together with the difference principle than by any alternative principles that directly aim at equalizing the economic resources of all citizens. Rawls therefore has more resources than some might think to defend the claim that he has captured the central sense of 'freedom' at work in the ideal of citizens as free and equal.

As we have just seen, Rawls claims that equality in the rights and liberties of citizens is consistent with significant inequality in the resources citizens have: resources that are required for the exercise of these rights and liberties. At least, he claims this is true if we leave aside the special group of political liberties. In order to challenge this claim, one would have to show that Rawls' theory fails to protect in some important respect the status of citizens as free and equal. One way to do this would be to try to show that the non-political basic liberties have some comparative or relational aspect in the same way that the political ones do: that one's position relative to others is relevant in terms of the extent to which one can enjoy all the basic liberties characteristic of free citizens. Philip Pettit's neo-republican theory of freedom as non-domination can be used as a basis for developing such a criticism, although Pettit himself has not criticized Rawls on precisely these grounds. In the following section I will briefly present the main elements of Pettit's account of freedom as non-domination in order to determine whether this particular type of freedom can be adequately protected by Rawls' principles of justice. I will argue that freedom as non-domination captures a sense of freedom that is significant enough to require some adjustments to the application of the theory of justice as fairness and that it has the kind of comparative aspect that Rawls acknowledged as problematic in the case of the political liberties.

Freedom as Non-Domination

Philip Pettit has argued that there is a conception of freedom as non-domination that is distinct from both the negative notion of freedom as non-interference and the positive notion of freedom as self-mastery (or autonomy) that Isaiah Berlin famously distinguished.[15] Pettit's distinct understanding of freedom is present in the intuitive judgment that to be free, in contrast to being in the condition of a slave or a colonized nation, is to not be subject to the arbitrary will of another. It hardly needs argument that it makes perfect sense to say that the slave or the colonized nation lacks freedom. But many traditional accounts of freedom as non-interference or freedom as self-determination or autonomy cannot satisfactorily explain this judgment, at least in some cases. Consider: the slave may have a benevolent master who does not interfere in her life to any very significant degree. Nevertheless, she lacks freedom. Similarly, colonized people may be ruled by a benevolent despot who does not interfere in their lives even to the degree characteristic of a democratic government. Nevertheless, they are not a free nation. As regards their autonomy, slaves and colonized nations may be autonomous if autonomy is understood as some sort of capacity for self-determination that they have succeeded in developing in spite of their situation—though they would not count as autonomous under other conceptions that require the relatively unimpeded exercise of capacities for self-determination.[16] It is the relational situation of domination (which is consistent with a lack of interference and with an agent's possession of developed capacities for self-determination) that better explains the lack of freedom of slaves and colonized nations. Thus, Pettit calls his distinctive conception of freedom "freedom as non-domination." The central theoretical notion in Pettit's account—domination—can be understood as: "An agent A dominates another agent B to the extent that A is in a position to interfere arbitrarily in some of the choices and actions of B."[17]

For Pettit, there is a wide variety of actions—including coercion, threats, and manipulation—that counts as interference, since these actions "intentionally worsen an individual's choice situation." But of course not all interference is arbitrary. Pettit uses the expression "arbitrary interference" to mean "interference that is not subject to suitable controls." There are two quite different types of arbitrary interference, depending on whether the interfering agent is (a) a private individual or a private collective agent, or (b) the state. When the interfering agent is a private agent, A's interference in B's affairs counts as arbitrary whenever A can practice it at will and with relative impunity, when it is not controlled in a way that ensures that it tracks the individual interests and opinions of B. In contrast, if the interfering agent is the state, A's interference with B's affairs counts as arbitrary when it is not controlled in way that ensures that it tracks the common interests of citizens as a class.[18] With this understanding of domination in hand, Pettit's view is essentially that someone is free, in his sense, if she is not dominated.

In order to clarify the negative notion of freedom as non-domination, it may be useful to contrast it with the negative notion of freedom as non-interference. There is some obvious overlap in the situations that proponents of freedom as non-domination and those of freedom as non-interference would describe as situations in which people lack freedom: these are situations in which people suffer from actual arbitrary (or uncontrolled) interference. But the notion of freedom as non-domination makes room for the possibility of suffering interference that is not arbitrary and does not compromise freedom, as in the case of interference of appropriately established laws. In fact, even in such cases advocates of freedom as non-interference could agree with Pettit that such laws do not amount to a genuine loss of freedom, provided that the laws are justified in an appropriate way. A more significant difference between the two conceptions of freedom appears in the converse case, when one considers cases in which someone is dominated (that is, when someone is vulnerable to arbitrary interference), but in which that person is not suffering any actual interference. In such cases, theorists concerned with freedom as non-interference would be concerned with the degree to which it is likely that there will be actual interference, rather than with the structural relationship of domination itself. Thus, if employees are in a position to suffer arbitrary interference from their employers because of the risk of unemployment if they are fired, or if wives are in a position to suffer arbitrary interference from their husbands because they would be destitute if they divorced or because there are no well-enforced laws against spousal battery, a consistent defender of freedom as non-interference would be more concerned if such interference was statistically likely to happen. In contrast, Pettit views the structural relationship of domination as bad in itself. In his view, such relationships involve a loss of freedom even when the probability of the dominated person's suffering from actual interference is very low. A focus on the structural relationship itself allows Pettit to note that sometimes the absence of interference—or its low probability—can be explained by the activities of the dominated person, who may resort to strategies of seduction, avoidance, or ingratiation to make interference less likely. Different advocates of freedom as non-interference may make different assessments of these kinds of situations. Some may say that when people are led to strategic planning and to the adoption of servile behavior of this sort, they are in situations that resemble those in which someone is explicitly threatened. Such advocates of freedom as non-interference will be able to claim, with Pettit, that these situations compromise freedom. But others might say that since there is no explicit threat, these are not situations in which freedom is compromised. For example, this is the position that Isaiah Berlin would take.

Whatever the precise relation between freedom as non-interference and freedom as non-domination, it should be clear that concern with freedom as non-domination leads to a distinctive focus on inequalities of power as something that compromises freedom, at least when such power is not checked. If one accepts that the idea of freedom as non-domination captures an important sense in which people can be free, one important practical question is the following: What kinds of policies can best secure or promote this kind of freedom? Pettit claims that the best means for reducing the capacity for arbitrary interference by private parties is the rule of law, supplemented by policies of redistribution of resources that increase the bargaining power of vulnerable individuals. For example, well-enforced criminal laws serve to protect individuals from physical harm and threats of physical harm, divorce laws that establish rights to alimony and adequate levels of child support increase the bargaining power of women in traditional marriages, and labor laws that mandate holidays and benefits protect employees from entering into exploitive labor contracts. With regard to assurances against arbitrary interference by the state, Pettit's primary focus is on the design of political institutions. Among other beneficial effects, well-designed institutions can, by means of mechanisms of checks and balances, prevent the accumulation of power in a few hands. They can make use of regular elections to check the performance of public representatives. And they can make it easier for citizens to contest public decisions in a variety of ways, in order to make the law more responsive to their interests. However, there is a notable absence in Pettit's lists of suggested policies; nowhere does he advocate moral or political education. This seems to be a significant omission, given that well-designed educational policies may contribute to a wider and deeper general knowledge of the workings of the political system, to the development of the abilities required for making effective political demands, and to the cultivation of moral dispositions to act in ways that protect one's own interests and that respect the interests of fellow citizens. All of these potential results of educational policies promise to facilitate the processes that Pettit appeals to as means to the reduction of domination.

Justice as Fairness and the Prevention of Domination

With the presentation of freedom as non-domination in hand, we are now in a position to determine whether Rawls' principles of justice are capable of protecting citizens from domination both by private parties and by the state. If it is true that freedom as non-domination captures an important sense of freedom—one that ought to be included in the ideal of citizens as free and equal—a society that fails to protect its citizens from serious forms of domination could not plausibly count as just. I will argue that Rawls' understanding of the basic liberties as legal protections from interference in central areas of one's life comes very close to Pettit's understanding of freedom as non-domination. In my view, Rawls' conception of the basic liberties as protection of key areas of one's life is completely different from the caricature of freedom as non-interference that sometimes appears in the literature as the 'liberal conception of freedom.' This simplistic account of freedom as non-interference sees the law as a threat to freedom and takes 'greater freedom' to be virtually synonymous with 'more options for action.' One important feature of the caricature of freedom as non-interference is that it does not make any qualitative distinctions between the kinds of activities that individuals can engage in. It therefore also fails to make any corresponding distinctions regarding which kinds of interference are more serious. It counts any trivial restrictions on action as reductions of freedom. For example, in this view a detour on my normal route to work counts as a reduction of my freedom because I cannot go in my normal way. As per Rawls' understanding, this does not count as a reduction of basic liberty—not even as a trivial one—because driving on one street rather than another is not a central activity of citizens. Rawls' list of basic rights and liberties identifies the kinds of activities of citizens that should be protected.

Now, it is true that Rawls does not generally consider the reduction of citizens' freedom that is manifested in relationships of domination.[19] One reason for this is that his main concern is to justify an ideal theory of justice that assumes that citizens comply with the principles of justice and that there are no historical obstacles to the just functioning of social institutions.

Nevertheless, it is worth asking whether Rawls' theory manages, non-accidentally, to protect the freedom as non-domination of citizens. If justice as fairness is to secure the status of citizens as free and equal, it should protect them from the possibility of arbitrary interference by the state or private agents.[20] Our question can be split into two distinct sub-questions, reflecting the dual nature of Pettit's notion of domination:

1. To what degree are the choices of individual citizens protected from arbitrary interference by the state?
2. To what degree are the choices of individual citizens protected from arbitrary interference by private parties?

As regards the sort of freedom at issue in (1)—freedom as non-domination from the state—it should be fairly uncontroversial that the theory of justice as fairness adequately protects citizens via the basic rights and liberties. These are rights and liberties which are guaranteed by the political institutions; they are inalienable and the state cannot legitimately violate them. The only justification for allowing certain restrictions on the basic rights and liberties is that doing so is required to secure an adequate system of equal liberties for all citizens. Rawls thinks that a society cannot be just unless it is a democracy, the central social and political institutions of which embody the ideal of citizens as free and equal.[21] Granting all citizens the right to vote, to express their political views, to participate in a variety of political associations, or to engage in civil actions such as lawsuits serves to ensure that citizens are not dominated by the state.[22] Although Rawls does not enter very deeply into issues of institutional design, his discussion of the political liberties shows that he is aware of the need for an adequate design of political institutions.[23] Moreover, the theory of justice as fairness guarantees the fair value of political liberties. This guarantee is meant to prevent the richest from controlling the political process and over-representing their interests in state policy. Rawls acknowledges that when economic and social inequalities are too large, there is a risk that one part of society will dominate the rest by controlling the machinery of the state. He puts the point in the following way, explicitly using an intuitive notion of domination:

> When those kinds of inequalities are large, they tend to support political inequality. As Mill said, the bases of political power are (educated) intelligence, property, and the power of combination, by which he meant the ability to cooperate in pursuing one's political interests. This power allows a few, in virtue of their control over the machinery of the state, to enact a system of law and property that ensures their dominant position in the economy as a whole. Insofar as this domination is experienced as a bad thing, as making many people's lives less good

than they might otherwise be, we are again concerned with the effects of economic and social inequality.[24]

In my view Rawls' list of citizens' basic rights and liberties can be used to provide a plausible interpretation of Pettit's more indeterminate notion of the common interests of citizens—a notion that is essential to Pettit's account of state domination.[25] Moreover, the basic rights and liberties will be protected by law in a Rawlsian just society. Thus, in order to assess whether the state or particular laws dominate citizens, we can focus on the question of whether the state respects and upholds citizens' basic rights and liberties. It is, however, not enough that these basic rights and liberties are simply listed in the constitution. Rather, they must also be adequately protected by means of effective laws and adequate institutional design. This is not very different from Pettit's proposal for dealing with the problem of domination by the state. But Pettit avoids providing a list of basic rights and liberties of citizens, appealing instead to the idea that state interference should be checked in a way that is forced to track the common interests of citizens, whatever those interests turn out to be. When Pettit does consider the strategy of talking about the basic liberties of citizens instead of using 'liberty' as a mass noun, he decides that it is best to leave the basic liberties unspecified.[26] In place of an explicit list such as Rawls', he offers a number of conditions that a list of liberties must meet if it is to count as a list of basic liberties. For example, the liberties should be capable of being equally enjoyed, they should be important in the life of people, and they should be as extensive as possible. Despite this and other differences with Rawls, I take Pettit's work on the basic liberties as an acknowledgment of the merit of Rawls' proposal that we should select some particular liberties as the most significant.

Let us now turn to the sort of freedom at issue in (2): freedom as non-domination by private parties. At first sight, it might not be entirely clear whether the theory of justice as fairness manages to protect this type of freedom. Criminal law certainly protects individuals and groups from certain kinds of private interference, such as physical violence or threats of physical harm. But the theory of justice as fairness does not seem to protect individuals or groups from the full range of forms of private domination. This is because, outside of the political realm in which all citizens are considered equal, a Rawlsian just society might include highly unequal relationships of power in civil society and in the domestic sphere. For example, there could be relations of domination between husbands and wives (depending on what the law says as regards marriage and divorce), or between employers and employees (depending on the content of labor laws and the existence of unemployment benefits). But we should be cautious in claiming that Rawls' view allows such domination, because whether or not this is true depends crucially on how the prescriptions of the second principle of justice—both the fair equality of opportunity principle and the difference principle—are interpreted. I will argue that there is some textual support for an interpretation of the second principle of justice on which it functions to eliminate domination by private parties. But first let us examine the principle of fair equality of opportunity and the difference principle and some plausible readings that would leave the problem of domination unresolved.

As we saw in chapter 2, the principle of fair equality of opportunity requires that everyone should have the same legal rights of access to all desirable social positions. This means that there should be no legislation that enjoins different treatment to different groups, such as legal discrimination against women or an official system of apartheid. Moreover, the principle requires that individuals' life chances should not be determined by the social position in which they are born. Rawls claims that "those who are at the same level of talent and ability, and have the same willingness to use them, should have the same prospects of success regardless of their initial place in the social system."[27] If this principle is interpreted in a way that allows employers to practice informal forms of discrimination—say, by excluding women or racial minorities from jobs due to a prejudice that they are not committed workers—then the principle would not prevent the domination of members of these groups. Of course, one might be able to argue that the principle requires non-discrimination laws and perhaps certain kinds of quotas in order to overcome patterns of historical prejudice.[28] Andrew Mason has suggested another problem with standard interpretations of the principle of fair equality of opportunity. Suppose that we assume that "qualifications and motivation for jobs" includes the ability to work extra hours at short notice, or to work 60-hour weeks. If so, then those with childcare commitments, who are unable (or unwilling?) to work under those conditions, will not count as "equally talented and motivated." If we think of things in this way, then there is no transgression of equality of opportunity if their life chances are worse than others'.[29] This interpretation denies that women's limited access to many desirable social positions is a sign of their being dominated in society. Instead, it construes their situation as the result of their life choices. Later I will argue that this is the wrong interpretation of Rawls.

As regards the difference principle, it is quite indeterminate in its policy implications, both in ideal and in non-ideal circumstances. It is, after all, extremely difficult to establish which set of rules for the functioning of economic institutions will make the life expectations of the worst-off representative individuals as good as possible. It would be controversial, even among social scientists and economists, what set of taxes, market regulations, and other programs would work to increase the lifetime expectations of the least advantaged so that they could be fully participating members of society on an equal standing with the more advantaged. But the difference principle requires precisely this: that the life prospects—in terms of access to income and wealth and other social primary goods—of the least advantaged working members of society be maximized, understanding 'least advantaged' to refer to those with the fewest marketable skills. But the indeterminacy of the difference principle is just one problem. On some plausible interpretations of the difference principle, it is not violated if women do not do paid work, or do not have an independent source of income, and are consequently in a position to be dominated by their husbands. It may also be possible for employers to have such a high degree of power over employees that it amounts to a form of domination, on the plausible assumption that it is not always easy for employees to leave their jobs and find another source of income when they are not satisfied with their present working conditions. If one puts emphasis only on maximizing access to economic resources, the fact that employees suffer from domination may be overlooked when one assesses alternative methods of structuring the workplace.

All the foregoing might suggest that Rawls has little to offer by way of reducing private domination, at least by reference to the second principle. However, Rawls' remarks on a property-owning democracy belie this suggestion.[30] The idea of a property-owning democracy involves the widespread distribution of land and capital, laws limiting intergenerational transmission of property and wealth, and governmental policies that promote equality of opportunity in education. Richard Krouse and Michael McPherson argue that fair equality of opportunity in education would equalize the acquisition of human capital and would increase the number of people with marketable skills, leading to a reduction in the income generated by possession of such skills. The result would be the equalization of the difference in earnings between the more favored and the least favored income groups.[31] Because the system of a property-owning democracy prevents excessive concentration of economic power, partly by supporting intergenerational redistribution of property, it provides an obstacle to the formation of interpersonal relationships of domination that are based on socioeconomic inequality. Moreover, widespread access to education and training will mean that more citizens are capable of supporting themselves, and this will impede the formation of interpersonal relationships that lack viable exit options.

I would like to make a few remarks regarding the problem of the private domination of women, since it matters for our purposes that the second principle of justice not allow the systematic domination of women as a group. This is a topic that cannot be adequately discussed in a short space, but Rawls' responses to feminist criticisms, which were briefly examined in chapter 4, point in the right direction. It is worth stressing that Rawls clearly indicates that the principles of justice should operate to prevent the systematic domination of women:

> Since wives are equally citizens with their husbands, they have all the same basic rights and liberties and fair opportunities as their husbands; and this, together with the *correct* application of the other principles of justice, should suffice to secure their equality and independence.[32]

Rawls acknowledges that women have traditionally borne a disproportionately large share of childcare responsibilities, and that they have been seriously disadvantaged by divorce laws. He also sees that the childcare work done by women should be financially rewarded, and that divorce law should entitle women who have left the labor market in order to care for children an equal share of the increased value of a family's assets during the period the marriage lasted.[33] I would add that fair equality of opportunity for women also requires that there be policies that redistribute childcare responsibilities, as well as laws requiring the workplace to accommodate workers with young children.

The possibility of private domination must be taken into account when one tries to apply Rawls' theory to non-ideal contexts. In the real world, people sometimes resort to different forms of coercion, including threats and manipulation, in order to control the behavior of others. A thoughtful application of the difference principle should take into account the importance of dispersing power and protecting those who are vulnerable to serious forms of interference by others. It might seem that in order for a policy successfully to eliminate or minimize domination it must transform the structural relationships between individuals, so that it is not possible for any person to have unchecked power over another. We have seen such policies already: minimum wage laws, mandatory paid holidays and retirement savings, spousal support in case of divorce, and workplace accommodations and childcare support for workers with children, among others. However, there is a distinct, though complementary, strategy that has not been sufficiently explored in the literature.[34] This strategy focuses on encouraging the development of certain traits of character in citizens, so that they can avoid, resist, or contest relationships of domination, whether in their own case, or when they observe it as third parties. In the remainder of this chapter I will briefly discuss the ways in which schools might contribute to the reduction of domination in this way. I will further argue that the type of education I am proposing fits nicely within the political boundaries of a Rawlsian account.

Education for Freedom

As many readers will know, much has already been written on education for freedom. It may therefore seem likely that there are a number of readymade solutions to the problem posed earlier, of designing educational policy to minimize domination in non-ideal contexts. However, the existing literature on education for freedom tends to focus on the defense (or rejection) of a variety of conceptions of personal autonomy and on the ways in which personal autonomy might be promoted by schools.[35] These topics are sometimes discussed in the context of the problem of balancing the interests of children against distinct interests of their parents. That is, the problem on which such discussions primarily focus is the compatibility of educational practices that aim at the development of children's autonomy with parents' legitimate authority to make decisions about the education their children receive. Now, we have seen that Rawls' own theory of justice is committed to the protection of citizens' *political* autonomy, understood as their capacity to form, pursue, and perhaps revise their plans of life. This might seem to suggest that Rawls would favor requiring educational policies that promote children's autonomy. But Rawls explicitly rejects the political promotion of ideals of personal autonomy that would assert that some reasonable ways of living one's life are more valuable than others. In particular he denies that a good life must put emphasis on the critical examination of values, the pursuit of experiments in living, or the cultivation of individuality. Thus Rawls cannot hold that it is one of the legitimate aims of schools to encourage the development of these ideals. This is because the value of different ideals of personal autonomy is controversial. The only way to justify giving preference to them would be to prove that the stability of a just society actually requires that citizens satisfy one (or more) of these ideals. But in the absence of such an argument Rawls' commitments to the political justification of policies seem to preclude any endorsement of education for autonomy. However, Rawls' account of a just society would be defective if it condoned serious forms of domination: this would amount to undermining some citizens' status as free and equal. In this way, the case for educating citizens against domination is critically different from the case for educating citizens towards the cultivation of any ideal of personal autonomy. The positive value that reasonable people may give to ideals of personal autonomy can vary, since any such ideals will be controversial. But one can expect much wider agreement on the claim that domination is *prima facie* bad and that there are good reasons to avoid or prevent it (although of course reasonable people may sometimes consent to situations in which they suffer a certain amount of domination in order to avoid other more significant evils or in order to receive some compensating benefits). The reasonable expectation of widespread agreement regarding the badness of domination allows the case for the education for freedom as non-domination to be framed within the boundaries of political justification.

How might civic education contribute to the prevention of domination? Let us focus first on the threat of state domination. This involves the possibility that the state interferes in the lives of citizens in ways that are not checked so as to insure that interference takes their common interests into account. As we have seen, constitutional protection of the basic rights and liberties of citizens directly serves the goal of checking this sort of interference by the state, and ensures that laws and policies take these central interests into account. This goal can also be served by other aspects of the political system. For example, Pettit thinks that the existence of mechanisms that facilitate citizens' contestation of laws and policies helps to prevent state domination. But beyond these particular policies endorsed by Pettit, civic education can make a fundamental contribution to citizens' freedom as non-domination by the state. Knowledge of one's rights, together with a practical knowledge of the functioning of the political and judicial system, can be very powerful aids to making one's voice heard and to making one's interests count, particularly for those who belong to vulnerable groups.

There are a number of non-accidental features of Rawls' view that seem to support an educational policy that aims to impart civic knowledge. Rawls' inclusion in the first principle of justice of a guarantee of the fair value of the political liberties provides plausible grounds for justifying this type of civic education. Developing children's capacities to become effective political actors later in life contributes to the fair value of their political liberties. But it is not clear from Rawls' brief remarks on civic education whether, and to what extent, he thinks that schools should be required to teach students about the functioning of the political and legal institutions and about the procedures for contesting unfair policies. Many liberal philosophers seem to be quite confident that social institutions and associations other than schools will be sufficient to provide this particular kind of civic education, so that there will be no need for schools to go beyond teaching some elementary facts about the organization of government. And it seems very likely that Rawls shares this confidence. But reliance on such "invisible hand" mechanisms is, in my view, unwarranted. There are no guarantees that those who are most vulnerable to arbitrary interference—and who would profit most from having this type of civic knowledge because of their greater need to become effective political actors—will be among the ones who manage to acquire it outside schools. Certainly it is likely enough that the children of politicians or lawyers will acquire this type of knowledge at home. But the children of poor immigrant parents may not learn very much about the legal and political mechanisms that are available to protect their rights and to allow them to make their demands heard. It should be clear that this argument for encouraging the development of skills for political participation in schools does not assume that the good life requires political activities. Rather, it merely depends on the very plausible claim that political participation is an important means for the prevention of the domination of citizens, or groups of citizens, and for sustaining political institutions that are responsive to their common interests and concerns.[36]

Let us now turn to consider how civic education might help to reduce interpersonal domination. As Pettit understands domination, it is a structural relationship between two agents. Domination exists whenever one agent has the capacity to interfere at will and with impunity in some of the choices and actions of another, independently of the likelihood that the dominating agent will actually take advantage of this capacity, and interfere. In order to eliminate this kind of possibility of arbitrary interference between private parties, one needs to establish some mechanisms of checks and controls. One might argue that moral and civic education can obviously help reduce domination, because citizens who internalize basic moral norms would generally refrain from threatening, coercing, or manipulating the choices of others. That is, there is a sense in which the development of moral and political virtues might itself count as a check—albeit an internal one—on the possibility of arbitrary interference. Moreover, virtue need not only function as an internal check. If there are many citizens who have developed moral and political virtues, and if this widespread virtue is generally known to exist, then the possibility of informal social sanctions might also work as a check on arbitrary interference by private parties. It must be admitted, however, that reliance on personal virtues as the sole or primary means to promote non-domination in society is unrealistic. One reason for this is that we cannot expect that most people will be brought up to be virtuous in a very robust and reliable way. A system of just laws and well-designed institutions offers a better prospect for controlling interference by private parties than does an educational policy aimed at the cultivation of personal virtues. Nevertheless, personal virtues do play a necessary role as aids to the rule of law, and they may contribute to the prevention of at least some serious forms of private interference.

A second, and less well-explored way in which civic education might contribute to the reduction of private domination, or at least of the harms associated with being vulnerable to arbitrary interference, is by means of encouraging children to think of themselves as equal to others and as therefore entitled to respectful treatment. Among other harms, relationships of domination may generate servile behavior—sincere or not—in the dominated individuals. Such behavior may be a strategic response, designed to ingratiate oneself with a more powerful party. Or, worse, it may be the result of internalizing the message that one's own goals, desires, interests, and opinions do not and should not count as much as those of others.[37] But we need to specify more what servility consists in, since there are many competing accounts of servility and what is wrong with it, which lead to somewhat different educational recommendations.

The account of servility that I find most plausible follows a proposal offered by Thomas Hill, who characterizes servility as a vice.[38] Hill argues that servility involves misunderstanding one's rights as a moral person, or placing a comparatively low value on them in comparison with the rights of others. Calling servility a vice does not involve the assumption that all servile people are equally responsible for their attitudes. Some can certainly be excused by appeal to the circumstances of their upbringing or to the oppressive social environment in which they find themselves obliged to live. Among the examples that Hill provides in order to illustrate his account of servility, the most famous is that of the deferential wife, who believes herself to have a duty to serve her husband. As Hill describes the deferential wife, she believes that she must give priority to her husband's desires and interests, without thinking of herself as someone whose own desires and interests matter as much as his. In Hill's words: "To be servile is not simply to hold certain empirical beliefs but to have a certain attitude concerning one's rightful place in a moral community."[39] Now, one difficulty with this account of servility is the need for criteria that will serve to distinguish servile behavior from some forms of highly altruistic behavior. Some people give a very prominent place in their deliberations to the interests and well-being of others, with the result that they often sacrifice themselves for the sake of others. It seems plausible that at least some of these altruistic individuals do appreciate their equal moral standing and the fact that they themselves deserve respectful treatment. But how are we to distinguish these people from those who act in similar ways because they do not value themselves sufficiently highly? This is a real problem, and I do not have any detailed theoretical solution to offer. But I do think that in actual practice we can distinguish between these two kinds of people, and that our ability to do so somehow depends upon our ability to determine, by observing their behavior, whether or not they have a proper sense of what they deserve.

Let us return now to education against servility, with Hill's understanding of servility in mind. There are a number of ways in which education against servility may contribute to the reduction of domination and the harms associated with it. We have seen that one way to control arbitrary interference is by setting up laws and policies that protect individuals, particularly those who are most vulnerable. But even the most well designed of such mechanisms will fail to check interference if people are ignorant of their existence or if they lack either the courage or self-regard to use them. And in non-ideal circumstances such ignorance and lack of courage or self-regard are far from uncommon. Unjust social and political institutions often work in such a way that dominated individuals fail to perceive their equal moral standing. As a consequence, these individuals are not equipped to pursue their individual interests effectively or to demand the respectful treatment that they deserve. An example from Jean Hampton may help illustrate this point. Hampton takes her example from a novel by Zora Neale Hurston, set in the 1930s, in which a dying African American mother gives advice to her young daughter. The mother's advice is to get as much education as possible in order to avoid being under other people's power. This, obviously, expresses a straightforward concern that her daughter not be dominated. But the mother also, somewhat surprisingly, advises her daughter not to love anyone more than she loves herself. Hampton interprets this advice in the following way:

> This mother appreciates the extent to which her daughter's future ability to fend for herself, pursue her own interests, and have ambitions that she effectively achieves, is directly linked to the extent to which she believes in her own worth—that is, the extent to which she thinks she is someone who matters, whose talents are real, whose interests are important to satisfy, whose ideas and ambitions are something that others should take seriously.[40]

Because the daughter is a female and a member of a dominated group, she will repeatedly receive the message that her interests do not matter to the same degree as her "betters" and that her views do not deserve to be taken into account. Hampton argues that cultivating certain positive attitudes about her own moral worth can affect the way the daughter considers her interests and ambitions, and whether she will be prepared to pursue them later in life. What the example illustrates is the way in which developing a sense of one's own worth is tied not only to forming interests and desires, but also to one's beliefs about the kind of treatment that one can demand from others. This of course is not sufficient as an antidote to domination and its associated harms, given that there are limits to what a particular individual can do in such oppressive circumstances. But the example does show that one way in which domination can be perpetuated is by repeated messages that certain people's interests do not count as much as those of others. To the extent that these messages are internalized, they will render any mechanisms of contestation ineffective.

The foregoing remarks indicate one way in which schools could make significant inroads against domination: by encouraging boys and girls from all ethnic backgrounds to think of themselves as equals, and as entitled to form their own plans and to pursue them. Such a message will help them to resist social pressures 'to stay in their place.' If this kind of education against servility succeeds, then when children grow up they will be better able to avoid entering certain relationships of domination. Or, if they find themselves in such relations, the will be psychologically able to make use of any resources to make their voices heard. If all else fails, they will at least be more likely to exit such relationships altogether. One long-term result of such an educational policy might be that a majority of workers do not accept demeaning working conditions, and this might well have as a consequence a reduction of the level of domination in society. Similar claims might be made about women and their willingness to form marriages or interpersonal relationships that involve domination. But my case for education against servility is not based on the idea that such an education will have a tremendous social impact, especially if other social injustices continue. Rather, my argument is only intended to show that freedom as non-domination is an attractive political ideal—political in Rawls' sense of being capable of political justification—and that it should shape our educational practices in a distinctive and desirable way.

7 Patriotism

Patriotism in Rawls' Works

One theme running through this book has been Rawls' account of reasonable citizenship, which includes a set of moral capacities and dispositions. Another has been the need for a civic education that includes the teaching of a set of public principles and norms, as well the inculcation of a set of virtues that promote fair interactions between citizens who may not share comprehensive views of the good life. These political virtues include toleration, civility, and fairness, amongst others.[1] But a number of theorists have claimed that even this is not enough. They argue that a further requirement is that citizens share common feelings of identification with their society's institutions, history, and people. More particularly, some have argued that a Rawlsian account of justice, if it is to meet the requirement of stability, requires such feelings. In the present chapter I will examine these claims, and defend an account of the proper role for patriotism (or something close to it) in a Rawlsian theory of justice. The question will then be how a Rawlsian program of civic education can and should involve the cultivation of feelings of identification. Many of those who defend a program of patriotic civic education focus their attention on the teaching of history. I will argue that their proposals have serious problems, and that the proper place to try to inculcate the relevant forms of identification will be in something more similar to traditional 'civics' classes. It will be an open question whether or not the resulting account of civic education deserves to be called 'patriotic.'

Following Eamonn Callan, let us define patriotism as "an active identification with one's particular nation as a cross-generational political community whose flourishing one prizes and seeks to advance."[2] Some authors attempt a more fine-grained, normatively loaded definition by distinguishing between malign and benign forms of identification, and reserving the term 'patriotism' for the benign form and 'nationalism' for the malign form. This results in a somewhat artificial contrast between patriotism and nationalism. Another way of drawing a distinction between patriotism and nationalism might seem to become important when discussing policies for multinational societies in which cultivating identification with the existing political community is different from cultivating identification with a particular nation. But this way of drawing the contrast can become blurred in practice, since some defenders of nationalism propose creating 'wider' national identities even in such cases. For example, David Miller recommends cultivating a British national identity that would include English, Welsh, Scottish, and Northern Irish identities.[3] This nationalist proposal is essentially the same as the proposal Charles Taylor recommends under the name of patriotism, for Canada: finding policies that promote an identity that would subsume a plurality of feelings of belonging to different nations that are nested within a single but significantly decentralized state.[4] In contrast with the first, normative way of drawing the boundaries of patriotism, I leave open the question of whether patriotism is, overall, good or bad. With regard to the second, I leave nationalism to the side in this chapter, and focus on patriotism understood as identification with a people that has its own institutions of self-government.[5]

However one understands patriotism, its status in Rawls' theory of justice as fairness is neither clear nor explicit. There are no references to patriotism in the indexes of Rawls' books, nor is the topic explicitly discussed. Rawls works with a simplified model of a closed society. Such a society is by definition isolated and self-contained. Its citizens enter by birth and exit by death. One result of these simplifying assumptions is that certain questions, such as the question of what justice requires as regards recent immigrants, cannot even be so much as raised without having first to modify the theory.[6] In light of these same simplifying assumptions, it is not at all surprising that Rawls does not raise, much less answer, the question of whether it is desirable that citizens of a just society be patriotic, or the question of the attitudes that it would be desirable for citizens to adopt towards other societies or towards foreigners. When Rawls discusses the kind of deep commitments of citizens that contribute to the stability of a just society, he asserts that citizens should affirm the values of political justice, values that are embodied in political institutions and social policies.[7] Rawls thinks that it is important that citizens see themselves and their fellow citizens as free and equal, as bearers of certain rights, and as responsible for their ends and claims. These normative beliefs help to explain the behavior of citizens, their political participation and their fulfillment of other civic duties. Although the widespread acceptance of these political values has its initial source in the political culture of a democratic society, Rawls never says that citizens need to develop patriotic feelings of identification with the people to which they belong and its shared history. What matters for Rawls is simply that citizens think of themselves as free and equal and that they support and further just institutions.[8] This is of course something that they can do in the context of the particular democratic society into which they were born. But it is equally true that they can do it in any other democratic society in which they happen to find themselves. At least this is true if they become naturalized citizens.[9] No attachment to a particular political community therefore appears to be a necessary element of citizens' self-understanding in the theory of justice as fairness.

Let us call the kind of account of civic identity described earlier the 'principle-based' account. Many authors have challenged this kind of account of the desired core commitments of citizens, or of "citizen identity," because it does not explicitly include ties and feelings of belonging to a particular political community.[10] Yael Tamir has developed what might be labeled the 'hidden boundary argument' against the principle-based account of civic identity. Tamir argues that many liberal theories of justice rely on a hidden patriotic or nationalist strategy to mark the boundaries of the political community and to decide who is to receive the benefits of democratic citizenship.[11] According to Tamir, liberal theories of justice assume the existence of democratic societies that are established in a particular territory, with borders, the members of which are selected primarily by birth. Such societies have redistributive policies that aim to benefit only members, and they extend the full complement of legal rights only to members. Taking these restrictions of scope as evidence, Tamir claims that the viability of a liberal theory of justice is parasitic on the existence of a sense of national belonging. But Tamir does not proceed to reject liberalism. On the contrary, she endorses the idea that citizens should support liberal principles of justice. But in her view the stability of just institutions requires something more than the kind of civic identity suggested by the principle-based account. In particular, it requires affective ties to the political regime that embodies the relevant principles, and ties to fellow citizens as participants in a common enterprise. In her words, a theory like Rawls' fails to explain

> the roots of social union, the social forces that keep society as a distinct, separate, and more significantly, a continuous framework. Rawls suggests that social unity and allegiance of citizens to their common institutions are founded on an agreement regarding some guiding principles of justice. But this agreement is too thin, and is insufficient to ensure the continued existence of a closed community in which members care for other's welfare, as well as for the wellbeing of future generations.[12]

Strictly speaking, one should not say that there is a *hidden* boundary in *A Theory of Justice*, since Rawls is explicit that he is working with a model of a closed society.[13] Moreover, Rawls' account of stability does include a theory of moral development that takes natural feelings into account. What is not clear, from Rawls' texts, is whether such natural feelings include patriotism. However, if Tamir and other defenders of patriotism or nationalism are right, affective ties to a particular political community should be taken to be a basic element of citizen identity. This would mean that liberal theories of justice should admit and value the kinds of feelings that stand behind such ties. And, perhaps, their cultivation should even be an explicit goal of the state's educational policies.

A good deal more argument would be required to get from Tamir's claims about the assumptions of many liberal theories to her conclusions about the actual value of patriotic or nationalistic feelings. And, in fact, I do not find claims about patriotic feelings being instrumental to the maintenance of just social institutions persuasive, particularly once we move out of Rawls' ideal theory. It is quite plausible that in Rawls' well-ordered society there might be a reliable connection between patriotism and the sense of justice. But things are different if one has in mind non-ideal institutions and circumstances. It is plausible, given a real-world context, that patriotic feelings are generally undermining of justice. Despite grounds for skepticism, Tamir's argument is interesting because it challenges liberal theorists to be more explicit about the scope of their theories and about the status assigned to patriotic ties and identifications. In fact, recent debates on global justice have made it clear that philosophers who endorse liberal principles of justice for democratic societies do not agree about the structure and content of principles of global justice, nor about the value of patriotic identifications. Any view on such matters will be controversial, and will need explicit defense.

Rawls' work on international justice provides some clues to his assumptions regarding the role of patriotic ties and identifications.[14] As an initial step in his argument for principles of international justice, Rawls develops an idealized model of countries that he calls "peoples." Peoples have, by stipulation, reasonably just governments that respect the human rights of their citizens and that are willing to interact fairly with other peoples. But what matters for our purposes is that Rawls describes peoples as united by a feeling of "common sympathies" or common nationality that predisposes their members to cooperate and to desire to have a common government. In other words, Rawls' peoples are nations with just or at least decent governments.[15] We ought not read too much into this idealized model, but at the very least the model strongly suggests that for Rawls patriotic feelings of identification with one's political community are important for sustaining just political institutions. Otherwise, there would have been no reason for him to have stipulated that peoples are united by a sense of national belonging. It would have sufficed to have said that peoples have just governments. Indeed, this simpler way of putting it would have made room for the idea that multinational states can be just and stable: a possibility that Rawls does not deny. But he seems to think that the most favorable conditions for the maintenance of just institutions are those in which citizens identify with one nation and its state. At the very least we can say the following: he never mentions multinationalism as a possible political structure for a people.

How should we view the assumptions that Rawls makes about peoples? Are they merely simplifying assumptions that help us to focus on the most significant issues? Or are they the expression of significant theoretical commitments? Taken as empirical premises, it is simply false that states are unified political communities, that citizens belong to one and only one state, and that identification with this state is their most important political identity. Most societies are multicultural and multinational, and their members hold a variety of overlapping and sometimes conflicting political loyalties and identifications. Moreover, the number of people with dual or multiple citizenships is growing, as a result of processes of immigration and changes in the rules for conferring and withholding citizenship—rules that vary from country to country and interact in complex ways.[16] Some scholars defend accounts of the relationship between the state and its citizens that make use of the simplified conception as an ideal to aspire to, rather than merely as a theoretical device. Given the way Rawls defines peoples for the purposes of theorizing about global justice, he seems to think that societies would be better off if they were unified by a shared sense of national or federal identity. But even if this is a correct account of Rawls, much remains unclear. For one can regard it as better in some way for a society to be more unified, without thinking that the state would be justified in taking any steps to promote such unification. That is, it might be better for Canada not to have the internal conflict that results from its multinational character, but it certainly does not follow from this that it would be a good idea to try to eliminate national differences, or to promote Canadian patriotism. Moreover, despite Rawls' apparent approval of patriotic identification, it is not clear what specific contribution such identifications make, in his view, to the achievement of social justice. For it remains the case that what he offers as the key commitments of citizens are the following: an endorsement of the principles of justice and a view of all citizens as free and equal. It is these, in his view, that are necessary for the stability of just institutions.

Patriotism and the Sense of Justice

Eamonn Callan has proposed an influential defense of the idea that we should introduce patriotic feelings into a full presentation of Rawls' theory of justice as fairness. As Rawls acknowledges, the stability of a just society depends in large part on whether those who grow up under its just institutions are capable of acquiring an effective sense of justice. In connection with this requirement, Callan takes seriously the account of moral development Rawls offers in *A Theory of Justice*. But Callan also argues that patriotic feelings are a necessary step in the developmental process that leads to the full possession of a sense of justice. In order to understand Callan's suggestion, it will be useful here to briefly summarize Rawls' main points about moral development. In Rawls' account the development of moral capacities follows a sequence of three stages: the morality of authority, the morality of association, and the morality of principles. In the stage that is characterized by a morality of authority, feelings of love for their parents lead children to endorse precepts and norms given by their parents. As they move on to the morality of association, children and young adults understand and endorse a variety of increasingly complex norms that form schemes of cooperation, aided by feelings of friendship and trust towards other participants. These schemes may be as simple as games, or as complex as the regulated activities that take place in schools. Rawls claims that the morality of association includes the role of citizen. As he puts it:

> Thus we may suppose there is a morality of association in which the members of society view one another as equals, as friends and associates, joined together in a system of cooperation known to be for the advantage of all and governed by a common conception of justice. The content of this morality is characterized by the cooperative virtues: those of justice and fairness, fidelity and trust, integrity and impartiality.[17]

Finally, when young adults have acquired a sense of justice, they move on to the final stage, which involves a morality of principle. At this stage they are capable of acting according to principles of justice, even in the absence of favorable feelings towards the beneficiaries of their actions. Rawls thinks that the morality of principle follows naturally as a final stage after the morality of association, because in complex schemes of association participants learn how to adopt the point of view of others and how to strike appropriate balances between competing claims. Of course, on many occasions feelings of trust and care accompany just behavior, even for those who have reached the final stage of moral development. But the important features of the final stage are an understanding of the requirements of justice and the motivation to pursue them even when feelings push in the opposite direction, for instance, when one's peers do not share one's point of view.

Callan argues that the final step *within* the morality of association implies the acquisition of patriotic feelings that facilitate adopting the role of citizen:

> Induction into the role of citizen and the growth of affective attachment to fellow citizens are essentially tied to the particularity of the polity within which moral learning occurs: it is *this* scheme of just social cooperation to which the individual becomes attached, *these* fellow citizens with whom bonds of trust and affection take root. The only alternative interpretation is to suppose that in the morality of association individuals become attached to just schemes of cooperation in general and to all who might conceivably participate in them. But that is as absurd as supposing that within the morality of authority children become attached to loving parents in general, as opposed to the particular ones who love them.[18]

For Callan, identification with the role of citizen requires the support of—indeed, is partly constituted by—patriotic feelings: feelings of attachment to the particular political community in which one was raised as a child.[19] Such feelings help facilitate the development of attitudes of generalized concern for people whom we do not personally know. Patriotic feelings also provide motivation to support just schemes—something that is distinct from merely behaving justly, and which therefore seems to require a source of motivation beyond even a deep desire to behave justly. For instance, patriotic feelings of attachment might motivate political participation with the common good in mind. Or they might facilitate productive political debate by reducing distrust among participants who happen to hold conflicting comprehensive views about the good, or who have different ethnic or cultural affiliations. Finally, patriotic feelings might make people more willing to make sacrifices for compatriots. For example, they might lead them to support redistributive policies that secure access to education, health care, and other social benefits for fellow citizens. Callan thinks that patriotism involves concern for the justice of the particular political community one belongs to, in such a way that the realization of one's life plan is intermingled with a common fate shared with fellow citizens. This sense of shared fate explains why the demands of justice are not perceived as requiring a sacrifice but are seen as part of the search for one's own good.

Callan's account of the role of patriotic feelings in moral development does not imply that such feelings are the only source of motivation to behave justly. Nor does he assume that concern for one's country trumps other considerations.[20] The morality of association is to be followed by the morality of principle, which makes moral motivation more independent of feelings, and encourages impartial assessments of the interests of everyone affected by a country's policies. In this sense, a patriot with a sense of justice would neither support nor condone unfair policies towards foreigners even if such policies benefited her own country. Indeed, it would be problematic if patriots did not evolve beyond the morality of association and acquire a true morality of principle.

It is worth noting that Callan's interpretation of moral development implies more than the claim that patriotic feelings provide an important source of motivation that contributes to just action. His interpretation implies both that it is not possible to acquire the morality of principle without first passing through the morality of association, and that the morality of association includes patriotism as its last step. In my view, the sequence that Callan proposes is plausible, in the sense that it might correctly describe the moral development of some people. But the plausibility of this claim is not enough to prove that patriotic feelings are a precondition for the acquisition of the sense of justice. Let us grant, for the sake of argument, that it is true that there is a unique sequence of stages of moral development, and that this sequence requires a bridge between (a) feelings of endorsement to particular just schemes of cooperation that benefit us and our loved ones, and (b) impartial feelings of endorsement of just schemes in general. Even if this is all true, it is not necessary that, among the feelings mentioned in (a), there should be feelings of attachment towards a particular political community at the level of a (multi)nation state. That is, it is possible that growing up surrounded by the love and concern of a just family, and benefiting from participation in just associations of many different sorts may be sufficient to allow one to appreciate the ideal of fair social cooperation, without any need of patriotic love as an intermediary.

A second problem with Callan's argument is that it depends on a conception of moral psychology whose empirical adequacy has—to put it mildly—not been proven. This is a problem that is inherited from Rawls' speculative account of moral development, which Callan modifies to include patriotic identifications. But Rawls' account was only meant to provide a plausible story of how ordinary human beings might acquire a disposition to follow the principles of justice. His goal was to show that the principles do not impose psychologically unrealistic demands. Now, Rawls' account of moral development in *A Theory of Justice* is incomplete in the sense that it does not explain how citizens become aware of the existence of reasonable disagreements and of what he calls 'the burdens of judgment': a collection of factors that explain why such disagreements can be expected to arise and persist even among reasonable people. Of course, Rawls only begins to emphasize the fact of reasonable disagreement in his later work, so we cannot expect that his earlier account of moral development would explain reasonable citizens' attitudes towards such disagreement. But the fact of pluralism is central to Rawls' later theory. And this very fact suggests that there may also be a variety of ways of building a bridge between concern for particular others and impartial concern for justice. Many different religions teach at least some moral rules that apply impartially, as do universalistic philosophies.

Now, even if the empirical evidence definitively undermined Callan's account of patriotism as a necessary step in moral development, it might still be true that patriotic feelings reliably make an instrumental contribution to the achievement of social justice. However, as Margaret Moore has persuasively argued, the empirical evidence that might be taken to support a causal link between patriotic feelings and just social institutions is at best ambiguous.[21] Social scientists might investigate many different societies and try to come up with comparative estimates of levels of patriotic feelings and levels of social justice, in an attempt to establish correlations between them. But given the complexity of the phenomena, it would be difficult to come up with tractable measures that would yield compelling evidence one way or the other. Moore helpfully reminds us that the relationship between patriotic feelings and social justice is unavoidably complex because there are large bureaucratic, political, and legal structures that mediate between the two. And bureaucratic structures maintain redistributive policies in a way that is substantially independent of the feelings of citizens.

Let us suppose however that despite Moore's points it could be established that there was *some* causal link between patriotic feelings and certain kinds of civically useful behavior. This in itself would not show that patriotic feelings were, overall, instrumentally useful. For, as Harry Brighouse has pointed out, an assessment of the overall instrumental value of patriotic feelings needs to take into account not only the possibility of beneficial effects, but also the possibility of harmful effects. Certainly we can envision an enlightened patriotism that is oriented by a sense of justice in the way that Callan wants. But the existence of this possibility does not give us any reason to believe that versions of patriotism encouraged by existing states are or would be valuable (or even acceptable) from the point of view of justice.[22] The success of the instrumental argument for patriotism as a realistic and viable means for securing justice depends, to a great extent, on empirical facts. We cannot come to any justified conclusions about the overall beneficial or harmful consequences of patriotic identifications without information about very complex causal relationships. Moreover, even if we could obtain this kind of reliable empirical evidence, we would still have to make difficult normative assessments of the relative significance of the different sorts of beneficial and harmful consequences that we had predicted.

Patriotic Identifications and the Teaching of History

At this point one might be tempted to conclude that, because there is so much uncertainty regarding the instrumental value of patriotic identifications, we are in no position to decide whether a Rawlsian account of civic education should aim to cultivate patriotic feelings. On the one hand, if patriotic identifications help to mitigate the divisive trends of pluralism and facilitate agreement on political principles of justice, it would be *prima facie* good for schools to encourage them.[23] On the other hand, educational policies that aim to cultivate patriotism may encounter resistance from minority groups. Members of such groups may tend to see such policies as attempts to force assimilation. And this may be a reasonable view if, historically, their parents or other forebears have suffered as a result of oppressive policies of nation building.[24] Moreover, even if it were possible to instill patriotic identifications in a way that contributed to social unity and was inclusive of minority groups, the process of producing these patriotic attitudes might have an unfortunate tendency to distort citizens' understandings of their own country's obligations of justice towards other societies.[25] Despite all these worries, a brief critical survey of some proposals for patriotic civic education may yield some clues as to whether or not it is advisable even to try to instill patriotic feelings in schools. It may also lead us to question some assumptions regarding the particular means that are standardly envisioned.

Let us take stock. Up to this point we have been following Callan's definition of patriotism as identification with one's nation as a political community that extends across generations; generations that are united by a sense of common history. In this understanding of patriotism, patriotic identifications are identifications with a people that have a particular culture and particular political institutions. If one asks what sorts of commitments and identifications schools should attempt to cultivate in children, Callan will include patriotism as a central goal (though, of course, the patriotism he advocates will be tempered by ideals of justice and democracy). In contrast with this, Rawls' brief recommendations for the education of citizens do not mention anything like Callan's patriotism. With regard to the core of citizens' identities, Rawls' account seems to take identification with political principles of justice to be more important than identification with any actual historically defined people. But advocates of the instrumental argument for the teaching of patriotism will say that the patriotic identifications with which they are so concerned function as a source of cohesion for pluralist democratic societies. And they will argue that patriotism, together with other factors such as well-designed institutions, contributes to the achievement of social justice. For this reason Callan advocates a patriotic education, which, in his view, will establish general social and psychological conditions in which behavior in accordance with justice is more likely to take place.[26]

Let us turn now to the question of which particular subjects should play the central role in a curriculum that will promote patriotism. In answering this question, advocates of patriotic civic education tend to agree on the special suitability of history.[27] What they generally propose is that history be presented in such a way as to be civically engaging. In fact, this is already the way in which the teaching of history in schools is being conducted in many countries, both in the past and in the present.[28] The most common way of encouraging patriotism in history classes has been to present a rather mythical and glorious version of the past. Unsurprisingly, these 'improved' versions of history are more inspiring than versions that try to give an accurate view of what actually happened.

Despite its prevalence in actual practice, it is relatively rare for a scholar who favors the teaching of patriotism openly to endorse the mythological version. One well-known exception to this rule is William Galston.[29] Galston argues that the central aim of civic education is to mold the character of the youngest members of society so that they become supportive of their political community. Galston is aware that there is a tension between educating children to be loyal to a particular political community and encouraging them to develop and exercise their capacity for rational inquiry and thirst for the truth. In his view, civic education should be designed to teach students about central aspects of their own society in particular, since the goal is to develop a particularistic loyalty to it. Of course it would be optimal if this could be done while at the same time teaching children methods of critical inquiry. But Galston sees that an impartial search for the truth may have corrosive effects, undermining "structures of unexamined but socially central belief."[30] He is therefore willing to give up the more intellectual aspects of the teaching of history, and instead, in an often quoted passage, recommends a moralizing approach:

> On the practical level, very few individuals will come to embrace the core commitments of liberal societies through a process of rational inquiry. If children are to be brought to accept these commitments as valid and binding, it can only be through a process that is far more rhetorical than rational. For example, rigorous historical research will almost certainly vindicate complex 'revisionist' accounts of key figures in American history. Civic education, however, requires a more noble, moralizing history: a pantheon of heroes who confer legitimacy on central institutions and are worthy of emulation.[31]

On the view expressed in this passage, the teaching of history in schools is meant to provide a 'usable past' for molding students into citizens who are willing to make sacrifices for their society.[32] Galston thinks that civic education fails if it does not mold students into good citizens who support their political community and who believe in the legitimacy of its social and political arrangements. And it is his view that a rhetorical pedagogy is far more effective for shaping the beliefs and attitudes of the majority of students than one focused on the pursuit of truth by means of critical reflection.

It seems to me clear that Galston's approach is worrisome in a number of ways. Nor am I alone in my suspicions. One of the best criticisms of this sort of distorted patriotic history comes from Eamonn Callan, who argues that teaching Galston's brand of patriotic history would lead, if successful, to morally debilitating effects on students' characters.[33] Callan claims that such an education is dangerously likely to impair students' capacity to understand and assess both the past, and current social and political issues. The main cause of these effects, according to Callan, is that such a civic education would encourage students to believe in simplifying fictions that are more comforting than the real facts of their societies' past and present. That is, teaching history in this way would generate a propensity to filter complex political issues and unpleasant truths into a set of bland and uplifting patterns, leading to self-deception. I think Callan is right in all this. But Callan seems to think that at least part of the harm of a distorting history is a direct harm to those who are deceived. That is, there is something intrinsically bad about living in a state of self-deception. But I would not like to rest my criticism of Galston on this normative claim. In fact, *prima facie*, there is something good about being comforted and in feeling part of a great political tradition. I do not think that there is any persuasive argument to show that the lives of people who believe in pleasant patriotic myths would be worse. Certainly it is not likely that such beliefs would make them delusional as regards other facts more closely related to their personal well-being.[34]

My own view is that the main harms caused by a deliberate distortion of history for the sake of promoting patriotic feelings will not be direct harms to those who receive such an education. Rather, they will be harms to the health and stability of democratic institutions. An education that makes use of such distortion, if it were successful, would deprive society of citizens who could monitor the policies of their own government, since it would make it very hard for them to determine how they should act if their government decides to adopt policies that are seriously unjust. Given that in a non-ideal world there is always some risk of governments veering off course in this way, it is not advisable to try to shape citizens' character in such a way that they are obedient to authorities and either unwilling or unable to evaluate the policies those authorities are implementing. Recent history supplies innumerable examples with which we might illustrate this point. For purposes of argument it may be most useful to focus on cases in which governments adopt unjust measures against their own citizens, rather than on cases of injustice against other societies. In this way, we can avoid the difficulties involved in the assessment of the particular claims by different parties in international conflicts. With this in mind, one striking example can be found in Argentina's recent past.[35] Between 1976 and 1983, Argentina was governed by a military dictatorship that was responsible for the kidnapping, torture, and killing of roughly 30,000 people. The heads of the military government, who were primarily responsible for these crimes, attempted to justify their actions as part of a war against subversion that was threatening the core values of the nation ('the Western and Christian way of life'). Sadly, during the war with the United Kingdom in 1982, the military government had ample support from the general population. In part, this support can be explained by a shared conviction among Argentineans of indisputable rights over the Malvinas/Falkland Islands preached in history handbooks and consistently taught to each new generation.[36] Of course I do not mean to suggest that Galston would endorse any of these governmental policies, or that he would hold that good citizens would support such a government. Rather, my point is that the sort of moralizing civic education his account advocates provides inadequate resources for the prevention of a dangerously uncritical support for illegitimate or unjust governments. Even those who live in societies with reasonably just governments backed by a long democratic tradition should not take the justice and stability of their political system for granted. Even democratically elected governments may suspend or violate some of the civil rights of their citizens. Or, more often, they may completely ignore the human rights of non-citizens: for example, by torturing foreign prisoners. Inculcating a patriotism that is essentially divorced from the development of critical capacities makes it more difficult for citizens to make an impartial assessment of their governments and to decide to oppose unjust policies. The risks of generating uncritical support are even greater when one turns to consider the likelihood of opposition to unjust governmental policies that affect other countries, rather than one's own compatriots.

Because the teaching of mythic versions of the past has so many liabilities, most advocates of patriotic history endorse the teaching of a more truthful version—of course, one that is appropriate to the students' age. A truthful presentation of the past allows for better historical analysis, and this amounts to a better education for children, both in terms of acquiring knowledge and of developing capacities for sound political judgment. Now, since there really is no such thing as the 'accurate historical account,' the best one can do is to try to present a representative variety of fairly reliable points of view; by this I mean not merely the point of view of different historians, but the points of view of the various historical groups affected by the issues of the day. This method for informing students about complex historical events certainly makes more room for a discussion of the possible causes of such events and of the roles played by different historical actors: women, ethnic minorities, and the working classes.[37] After all, the history of a country includes much more than the mere history of the actions of the government and working of the economy. By bringing in a variety of points of view, and by presenting different interpretations of historical events and their causes, teachers could discuss the distinction between reasonable and unreasonable disagreements. In fact, the mere presentation of the history might manage to do this, even if teachers did not emphasize it. In this way, the study of the past would not be that different from the study of current social and political issues, which often include disagreements that can be explained by what Rawls calls the burdens of judgment. And this is an important benefit, since Rawls requires reasonable citizens to be aware of these burdens.

However, for those who wish to make the teaching of history a means for cultivating patriotic sentiments, the following problem remains: truthful stories are not guaranteed (or likely) to be as patriotically uplifting as myths. In my view, one significant difficulty that advocates of truthful patriotic history face is practical: how to encourage patriotic identifications while teaching history with integrity.[38] That is, the question is how to be inspiring in the right way without covering up the personal failures of political leaders; the innumerable instances of cruelty, greed, and ambition leading to pointless wars; the enslavement of entire peoples; and injustices of other sorts. Those who endorse a more truthful but still patriotic approach to the teaching of history are by no means unaware of these difficulties. Despite this, they still believe that students can be encouraged to make 'the best of the tradition' by selectively emphasizing certain aspects of the history of the nation of which they are supposed to be inheritors. But I think they are overly optimistic. It is already a challenging task to give students a clear sense of how complicated actual historical events were. It is even more challenging to do this while also finding something valuable in what is studied—and valuable in a way that inspires some sort of identification with the nation. I do not think that teachers can be asked to do this. Despite its widespread actual practice, and despite the fact that it is advocated by many educational theorists, history classes should not be used to promote patriotic identifications. Attempts to use them in this way tend to encourage the distortion of historical facts to make them more palatable and uplifting. Rather, history classes should try to impart essential historical knowledge and to develop students' abilities for historical research and interpretation. If they manage to pursue these goals, that will be enough of a contribution to their capacities for political judgment and appreciation of reasonable differences of opinion.[39]

Feelings of Identification and the Teaching of Principles of Justice

Should we conclude that it would be best simply to give up on the project of cultivating patriotic feelings of identification? The preceding discussion assumes that one central goal for Rawlsian civic education is that students acquire a sense of justice and appreciate the importance of the ideals of freedom and equality that are (imperfectly) embodied in the political institutions of their societies. The defenses of patriotism we have discussed share this assumption and therefore value feelings of identification only instrumentally, insofar as they help to develop the sense of justice. To proponents of these views, history seemed like the obvious choice as the proper location for patriotic civic education. Unfortunately, the problems with attempts to teach patriotic history seem insurmountable. But if the final goal is the development of a sense of justice, then there is a more direct route than patriotic history lessons. Instead of an oblique approach, a better strategy would be to teach students about philosophical principles of justice, the variety of arguments that may be used to support them, and how these principles might be embodied in the design of democratic institutions, policies, and laws. If the arguments are sound, they may well inspire the dispositions and attitudes of Rawls' reasonable citizens.

Admittedly, Rawls' principles of justice are rather abstract and might seem less inspiring than heroic tales of struggles for freedom and equality. But explaining what these principles involve can be made more concrete by appeal to examples of actual policies and laws that can be seen to be grounded in them, and this will be my suggestion. To clarify what is at stake in different proposals for civic education, let us distinguish three different kinds of identifications that such education may be designed to promote. Civic education may encourage students to identify with (a) principles of justice, (b) particular political institutions that embody principles of justice, or (c) the history of a people and of its political institutions.[40] In my view, it is only (c) that can properly be called patriotism, if we are using words with their normal meanings. My proposal is to try to encourage identification with (a) by means of teaching about (b). For example, teachers could examine the constitution of a country, or international human rights documents, that include protections of the basic rights and liberties contained in the first principle of justice. In order to get a sense of what is involved in these declarations of rights, teachers could also discuss some of the legal and political controversies over the proper interpretation of these rights and liberties. That is, they could discuss what it means to say that citizens have freedom of conscience, freedom of speech, or the right to a fair trial. It is more difficult to find examples that match the prescriptions of the second principle of justice perfectly. But legislation that prohibits discrimination in employment, or publicly funded school systems, might usefully be interpreted as (imperfect and partial) implementations of the principle of fair equality of opportunity.

Some may want to call the teaching of (b) 'constitutional patriotism,' since it is likely to involve something like an identification with the constitution of one's country and its central principles. Although I endorse an understanding of (b) that would give the constitution an important role, I would resist the patriotic label, and I would not focus narrowly on the constitution. The ordinary sense of 'patriotism' does not seem to me to be so intellectual, and does not put principles of justice center stage. Of course, teaching that there are valuable ideals that orient and justify the design of the actual political institutions and laws of a society may encourage students' sense of identification with those particular institutions (that is, with [b]). And this is a welcome result, in so far as it may help them feel at home with these institutions and take a more active role as citizens. But, again, this is not really patriotism as it is generally conceived. As Andrew Mason has pointed out, people may identify with their political institutions without necessarily identifying with a particular people or with the historical process that led to the creation and transformation of political institutions over time.[41] The history of political institutions—even good ones—is often as morally problematic as the history of the societies where they emerged. But as long as it is true that these institutions reasonably embody valuable political ideals in the present, it is appropriate to teach students about them. In fact, students should also be taught that there is a gap between political principles of justice and their imperfect embodiment in social and political institutions, so that their allegiance to such institutions is not unconditional but is regulated by their sense of justice. As to identification with (c), this seems to me inessential to good citizenship and to involve too many moral liabilities.

One might worry that I have not advanced much from my initial proposal for a Rawlsian civic education. This proposal centered on the teaching of public principles and norms, and the cultivation of political virtues. But at the very least, there is an important negative conclusion that we have reached: there is no good reason to think that the teaching of patriotism is instrumentally valuable as part of such an educational policy. Moreover, I have conceded to the advocates of patriotic civic education that it is unlikely that the principles of justice can be taught by means of philosophical arguments alone, without any reference to existing institutions and practices. Even political philosophers such as Rawls came to embrace their principles in part as a result of reflection on the actual history of democratic thought, and based on acquaintance with actual democratic institutions. In my view, the study of one's own country's institutions of government can be fruitfully combined with philosophical discussion and a normative assessment of those very institutions. In this way, even if this type of civic education tends to generate feelings of identification with particular political institutions, it will be inherently more likely to avoid the moralizing distortions of patriotic history.

8　Cultural Diversity

Pluralism and Cultural Diversity

Using Rawls' theory of justice as a theoretical framework, in chapter 5 I defended an account of education for citizenship that focused on the need to teach public principles and norms, as well as the political virtues characteristic of reasonable citizens. I argued that this educational proposal counts as political because its justification does not depend on comprehensive doctrines about the good. Instead, it depends only on political ideals that are present in the public culture of democratic societies. The fact that this proposal counts as political does not imply that it is minimalist in any way, or that it "stays on the surface," as Rawls' own remarks on the aims of civic education might suggest.[1] The reflective endorsement of political principles and democratic procedures almost unavoidably brings with it the cultivation and exercise of political virtues that are virtually certain to have a deep impact on citizens' character. As we have seen, education for reasonable citizenship encourages the promotion of virtues such as tolerance, mutual respect, and fairness, and discourages vices such as dogmatism, intolerance, racism, and the unrestricted pursuit of self-interest. Rawls admits that the teaching of political virtues will affect the relative likelihoods of different comprehensive doctrines being transmitted from one generation to the next, favoring the adoption of some and discouraging the adoption of others. In order to teach the political virtues and other dispositions that are characteristic of reasonable citizens—for example, an acceptance of the burdens of judgment—schools should attempt to foster knowledge and understanding of a variety of comprehensive doctrines. And they should attempt this even if such a policy generates some controversy. In other words, rather than adopting a policy of 'liberal silence,' civic education should acknowledge the fact of pluralism and make it an explicit subject of study in schools.

We have seen that defenders of liberal patriotism/liberal nationalism criticize Rawls' claims about the core commitments that citizens must have in order to ensure the stability of just social institutions. Rawls thinks (1) that citizens should see themselves and their fellows as free and equal and as bearers of certain rights. He also argues (2) that citizens should take responsibility for their life choices and the demands they make on society's resources. Further, he thinks (3) that citizens should be willing to cooperate with others on fair terms, and (4) that they should acknowledge the existence of reasonable disagreements regarding a number of empirical and evaluative issues. These four commitments are implicit in the claim that citizens should accept the validity of the two principles of justice as the principles that should regulate the functioning of the institutions that make up the basic structure of society. However, and as we saw in chapter 7, advocates of liberal patriotism/liberal nationalism argue that this 'principle-based' account of citizens' commitments is too thin. In their view, these commitments, on their own, would fail to motivate common citizens to a degree sufficient to support just social institutions (if they exist), or to work towards their achievement (if they do not). Appealing to a variety of considerations, they argue that what is needed to take up the slack is the cultivation of feelings of identification with one's particular people, including its history and political institutions. That is, they argue that such patriotic or nationalistic feelings are required to provide the additional motivation necessary for the achievement of enduring social justice.

Because Rawls uses a simplified model of a closed society when he writes about domestic justice, it is not clear what views he might hold about the need for or usefulness of patriotic feelings. One might speculate that, just as he relies on parents' and children's love for each other in the family to play a crucial role in the processes leading to the acquisition of a sense of justice, he implicitly relies on the development of feelings of patriotic love towards one's political community. This is Eamonn Callan's reading of the theory of moral development in *A Theory of Justice*, which I examined in chapter 7. In further support of Callan's reading, we can add that Rawls' later theory of international justice, as presented in *The Law of Peoples*, uses a model of countries that are in fact united by feelings of shared nationality. This suggests that such feelings, for Rawls, would somehow facilitate the stability of just or decent political institutions. But despite the plausibility of this interpretation, it remains true that Rawls never actually claims that patriotism is a requirement for the stability of just institutions. Nor does he ever explicitly include the cultivation of patriotic feelings among his educational recommendations.

Rawls agrees with liberal patriots/liberal nationalists on the importance of widespread acceptance of political principles. He also agrees with them on the value of political virtues and of feelings of identification. And although they focus on somewhat different sets of virtues and feelings, they all agree that certain virtues and feelings are required in order to provide a basis for unity in societies characterized by the fact of pluralism.[2] In Rawls' theory in particular, consensus on the principles of justice is the main source of stability among citizens, who might otherwise be divided by disagreements in the comprehensive doctrines about the good that they endorse (including religious doctrines), as well as by socioeconomic differences. In my view, teaching the core principles of justice should certainly be one of the central goals of civic education. But there is much more to be said about the guidelines and content of civic education. It is worth stressing that the theory of justice as fairness does not take into account a wide range of sources and sorts of social diversity, many of which may make it more difficult to reach consensus on principles, procedures, and policy in non-ideal societies.[3] In particular, Rawls makes it clear that his theory of justice is concerned with conflicts that derive from a plurality of comprehensive doctrines. He is explicit that he is not trying to deal with conflicts that stem from differences in ethnicity, gender or race.[4] As we have already seen, Rawls' ideal theory is built for a closed society, into which all citizens are born, and in which they live out their whole lives. In this way the theory uses a very simplified picture of society, ignoring the possibility that not all members speak the same language, that some are recent immigrants or that some members belong to national minorities.[5] Moreover, he stipulates that there are no historical obstacles to the just functioning of social institutions. The methodological decision to simplify his conception of society in this way comes at the cost of ignoring, for the purposes of political theorizing, pressing political issues that derive from the legacy of past injustices. These past injustices include slavery and legally imposed segregation, the killing and conquest of indigenous peoples, the persecution of national groups, as well as the many historical forms of women's oppression. In many societies, past injustices of this sort do a great deal to explain the existence of relationships of domination and enduring social divisions along ethno-cultural and racial lines in the present. These divisions can easily destabilize democratic institutions and complicate the prospects of achieving justice and legitimacy. Rawls says that these issues belong to "partial compliance theory," which tells us how to deal with injustice. He admits that

> Obviously the problems of partial compliance theory are the pressing and urgent matters. These are the things that we are faced with in everyday life. The reason for beginning with ideal theory is that it provides, I believe, the only basis for the systematic grasp of these more pressing problems [...] At least, I shall assume that a deeper understanding can be gained in no other way, and that the nature and aims of a perfectly just society is the fundamental part of the theory of justice.[6]

As we have seen, the fundamental part of the theory of justice consists of the two principles of justice. These principles help us assess whether a particular society is more or less just by directing our attention to the distribution of social primary goods among its members. The theory highlights the question of whether all members of society enjoy basic rights and liberties, whether there are policies that secure fair equality of opportunity irrespective of social background, and whether economic inequalities benefit the life prospects of the least advantaged.[7] When past injustices continue to have an impact in the present, in most cases part of that impact is represented in the failure of the society's basic structure to work according to the principles of justice. Some or most members of historically oppressed groups may not enjoy the basic rights and liberties to the same extent as members of privileged groups, or they may not have equal opportunities to access desirable social positions, or they may suffer from serious economic deprivation. The theory of justice as fairness points to the distribution of social primary goods as a way to compare and assess the situation of different individuals and groups, and recommends certain priorities for policy. Once a particular society has a certain basic quantity of available resources, the theory says that violations of the first principle of justice are more serious than violations of the principle of fair equality of opportunity and of the difference principle. It also assesses failures to promote equality of opportunity as more serious than economic inequalities (once a threshold of basic needs is satisfied).

So Rawls can, in many cases, rightly classify societies as unjust—including cases in which the injustices stem from historical factors. But what Rawls' theory cannot do is help us identify the causes of injustices in the distribution of primary goods, or the best policies for rectifying them. This is a task that requires additional knowledge of particular societies: both of their histories and of their present circumstances. The acquisition of this knowledge requires input from historians, sociologists, and other social scientists. Moreover, in order to provide detailed normative guidelines on public policy one has to address the difficult questions of partial compliance theory. That is, one has to modify the theory to take into account the existence of unjust institutions as well as unjust individual behavior. In this chapter I discuss some of the ways in which a Rawlsian account of education for citizenship might properly be extended to deal with the existence of wider forms of social diversity than mere diversity of comprehensive doctrines. In actual societies, many wider forms of diversity happen to be accompanied by different kinds of injustices, which fall within partial compliance theory. Injustices of this sort often cannot be explored fruitfully at the very abstract level of general theory, and require us instead to get into the details of the situation of particular societies. Before turning to the discussion of educational issues, some prior discussion of the place of 'culture' within Rawls' theory is necessary.

The Problem of Culture

There is no systematic examination in Rawls' works of the relevance of cultural differences to the question of social justice, or of the ways in which social policies should or should not take these differences into account.[8] Rawls' remarks on the fact of reasonable pluralism and its relevance to the justification of policies is not to be confused with a discussion of what we might call the fact of cultural pluralism or the fact of multiculturalism. Rawls' pluralism has to do with comprehensive doctrines, and these are simply different from cultures, though there are some interesting relations and interactions between them. Of course, to say that a culture is *not* a comprehensive doctrine is not to say what a culture *is*. And indeed there are innumerable definitions and uses of the notion of 'culture.' In order to make clearer the contrast between the fact of pluralism, as Rawls understands it, and cultural pluralism, it will be useful to narrow down our understanding of the notion of 'culture.' Following Jeremy Waldron, we can initially characterize culture in the following terms:

> "Culture" refers to a set of related practices and traditions associated currently and historically with a community—that is, with a human grouping larger than a family or a village, abiding longer than just a few generations, permeating the lives of its members in a constitutive way, and amounting in some sense to an *ethnos*, a people or a nation [...] The culture of a community is a way of doing things, particularly the things that are done *together*, throughout the whole course of human life: language, governance, religious rituals, rites of passage, family structures, material production and decoration, economy, science, warfare, and the sharing of a sense of history.[9]

Using this sense of 'culture' we can describe most societies as 'multicultural,' inasmuch as they contain more than one cultural community. A multicultural society, in the sense with which I am concerned, is one that contains more than one national group, or that contains groups of immigrants of different national origins, each such group having its own more or less distinctive set of practices and traditions.[10] However, the cultures of these groups tend to change over time as social conditions themselves change. Moreover, encounters between cultural groups unavoidably lead to mutual influence and some degree of transformation of their respective practices and beliefs. It turns out to be quite difficult to mark the 'borders' of particular cultures. This is especially true when cultural groups have lived in the same territory for an extended period and have spawned subcultures that have taken on lives of their own. Trade and communication technologies also contribute to the dissemination of the cultural materials and artifacts out of which cultural practices are sometimes constructed, and one result of this dissemination is that we may find significantly similar practices all over the world.

Even appealing only to this very general account of culture, it is easy to show that Rawls' fact of reasonable pluralism of comprehensive doctrines about the good is not equivalent to the fact of cultural pluralism. We have seen in chapter 3 that comprehensive doctrines include an organized set of values that make the world intelligible to people and that provide guidance in deciding which goals are worth pursuing, and how to balance them in case of conflicts. Even if people do not endorse a fully articulated comprehensive doctrine—such as one particular religion—we can still think of them as endorsing a conception of the good, that is, a set of ends or goals that they want to realize in life, which they think are valuable and worth pursuing. Whether we talk about a pluralism of comprehensive doctrines, or—in more simple terms—a pluralism of values in society, this does not amount to cultural pluralism. Cultures sometimes contain comprehensive doctrines, since most members of a cultural group may share a particular religion or worldview. But cultures could also be pluralistic. Cultures are not reducible to comprehensive doctrines or to sets of values. This is because 'culture' refers to the practices and traditions of groups, to their ways of doing things in the many realms of social life. These practices are no doubt permeated by the values of these groups, but they include many evaluatively neutral features as well.

The culture of a group is seldom chosen; rather, it is transmitted from generation to generation, so that those who participate in a shared culture learn to do things in ways that become 'second nature' to them. This is the case with the language that children learn, the stories and the music that they come to appreciate while they are growing up, the kinds of foods and ways of eating that they are familiar with, their ways of greeting family members and strangers, and many other things. This list of cultural practices should help to make it clear that in complex modern societies two citizens may share a culture without sharing a comprehensive doctrine about the good. Two citizens may endorse and live according to different comprehensive doctrines—one may be religious, for example, and the other agnostic—but speak the same language, follow the same social norms and conventions, and participate in shared social life more or less automatically, without having to think about how to do so. Conversely, two other citizens may share a comprehensive doctrine—they may both be Catholic—without its being at all appropriate to say that they belong to the same culture. One may be the remote descendent of English immigrants to the United States and the other a recent immigrant from Mexico. Their native languages, their acquaintance with the ways in which many social institutions function in the society in which they live, and whether they feel 'at home' there, will vary significantly, as will the ways in which they automatically deal with the many needs of everyday existence, such as when and what to eat, how to dress, what to read, and so on. These similarities and differences cannot be captured by Rawls' notion of pluralism of comprehensive doctrines, but they are still significant when it comes to the question of designing just social institutions.

In *Political Liberalism*, in a passage in which Rawls is discussing the basis of political authority, he seems to recognize the importance for most individuals of the culture in which they grew up. The passage offers additional evidence that cultural differences should not be reduced to differences between comprehensive doctrines:

... normally leaving one's country is a grave step: it involves leaving the society and culture whose language we use in speech and thought to express and understand ourselves, our aims, goals and values; the society and culture whose history, customs, and conventions we depend on to find our place in the social world. In large part we affirm our society and culture, and have an intimate and inexpressible knowledge of it, even though much of it we may question, if not reject.[11]

Here Rawls explains the importance, to most individuals, of their own culture, even when they do not endorse, as part of a comprehensive doctrine, many of its implicit values. This makes it clear that Rawls sees a distinction between culture and comprehensive doctrine. But the passage also suggests that Rawls is working with the assumption that each country contains only one culture. This is an obvious empirical simplification. Most contemporary societies are characterized by the fact of cultural pluralism, and the idea of culture therefore needs to be included, somehow or other, in any theory of justice that aims to provide policy recommendations. The question is: what kind of policies are required, permitted, or prohibited in response to the pluralism of cultural groups present in society?

What seems most uncontroversial is that a democratic society cannot pass highly coercive policies that would force its members into adopting the cultural mores and language of the group that happens to have the greatest political power, even if this group constitutes the majority in society. In the past, policies of 'nation building' did include highly coercive policies of this sort, that aimed at the forced assimilation of ethno-cultural groups (at least when they did not simply aim at marginalizing, enslaving, or exterminating groups seen as 'foreign' to the nation).[12] But there is wide consensus today that such policies are just as unjustified as the racist and ethnocentric assumptions behind them. However, there is not so much agreement about the positive proposals that would constitute an adequate response to the fact of cultural diversity.

Will Kymlicka stresses that there will always be significant pressures for assimilation in society, since social institutions tend to reproduce the culture of the majority. The strength of this tendency will depend on the number of groups the society houses, and on their size, territorial concentration, and relative amount of resources. But regardless of these matters, there will always be certain ways of doing things together that a majority of people will follow, without making any decision to follow them. The important point here is that even in a context of peaceful coexistence of cultural groups, some of these ways of doing things will be predominant and exert considerable non-intentional influence on others. For example, economic opportunities may be associated with learning the predominant mores and language, and the media may have a significant impact on the diffusion of customs and language, especially on younger generations. Kymlicka also points out that the state cannot avoid having significant influence on cultural practices. The political and legal system of a country can only function in one, two, or three languages at most, even though there may be translation services for trials, ballots, or other significant procedures. Political communities face decisions about the language(s) of instruction both in public and private schools, at each distinct level of the educational system. And the education provided by schools will unavoidably transmit certain cultural norms and values. Political communities also select what will count as the official holidays and symbols of the country or its regions, which again will reflect and enable the cultural self-understandings of some groups in preference to those of other groups. These and similar decisions concerning the operation of major social institutions play a significant role in cultural reproduction, affecting the prospects that the culture of a minority group will be transmitted to future generations. In order to answer the question of whether the state is permitted, or required, to take measures to support the culture of minority groups one must take these facts into account.[13] One must also consider the difficult question of what kinds of interests individual members of cultural groups have in the persistence of their cultural mores, as well as in their learning other ways of doing things and other languages.

Rawls never discusses these issues, and some critics infer from his silence that he would favor a policy of 'benign neglect' of cultures. But such a hands-off policy does not necessarily follow from his theory. In my view, his model of a well-ordered society operates with the simplifying assumption that there is a shared cultural community which is coextensive with the political community, which means that he is simply not trying to address the justice of the particular situations that national minorities and immigrants may face.[14] The issue cannot even arise in the societies he describes, so it is a mistake to infer anything from his silence on this issue. Rather, if we are to look to Rawls for some guidance on this topic, his theory will need to be extended by incorporating additional considerations.

Cultural Belonging and Social Justice

One way of extending Rawls' theory to address the situation of a subset of cultural minorities—national minorities—has been suggested by Will Kymlicka.[15] Kymlicka argues in *Liberalism, Community and Culture* that belonging to a cultural community with a shared language, history, and heritage, is a social primary good in Rawls' sense. In other words, belonging to a cultural community is a good that is essential if people are to be able to exercise their freedom to live according to their values. As we have seen, social primary goods are goods that serve as means to pursue a variety of plans of life, and that are fundamental for the development and exercise of the moral capacities of citizens. No matter what kind of plan of life people have, they also have a central interest in social primary goods. Cultural belonging has the status of a social primary good, or so argues Kymlicka, because no matter what the particular conception of the good a citizen should turn out to have, she will need to have access to a secure cultural context that will provide her with meaningful options and valuable activities to engage in. What Kymlicka has in mind when he refers to "a secure cultural context" is the continued existence of a cultural community which provides its members with the possibility of participating in social, educational, religious, economic, and political activities. Importantly, for a cultural community to be able to provide such options in modern conditions, the culture of the community needs to be "institutionally embodied" in schools, media, the economy, government, and so on.[16] Kymlicka offers this argument to support his claim that a liberal state should take measures to protect the cultures of national minority groups, such as indigenous communities and the Quebecois in Canada, to secure their continued existence. Significantly, he does not intend this argument to apply to immigrant communities.[17] He thinks that the state should treat the decision to immigrate as a voluntary decision to leave one's own culture behind and start a life in the context of a new culture. For Kymlicka, immigrants do not have a valid claim to the preservation of their culture, though they are entitled to respectful treatment and the accommodation of their practices in the institutions of the national majority of the country (or the province/state).

In Kymlicka's view, the appropriate measures to take in order to preserve the culture of national minorities will depend to a great degree on the situation of these groups. These measures range from providing financial resources and tax exemptions, to allowing the community to control the instruction provided in schools, to granting the community certain powers of self-government within a bounded territory. For example, it would be permissible for aboriginal communities to restrict who can live and vote in the territory they control, to have their own primary schools, and to have communal property of land. But these policies would not be permissible in Quebec. It would not be legitimate for Quebec to close its borders and prevent other Canadian citizens from moving into the province (unless they secede and become a separate country, which would grant them the same rights to control their borders as all sovereign states).[18] On the other hand, Kymlicka seems to think that Quebec can legitimately require that French be the language of instruction in most schools and that it can adopt a number of additional policies to secure the use of the French in other social institutions.[19]

As we have seen, Kymlicka recommends certain policies that will help ensure the continued existence of the cultural communities within a given state. Such proposals make room for cultural change, but try to give power to national minorities to control the direction of these changes, at least within the territory under their jurisdiction. Kymlicka stresses the fact that the members of a majority culture may take the availability of a secure cultural context for granted, and may not even notice the extent to which they rely on it. But members of national minorities sometimes face the risk that their cultures will disintegrate, making a host of everyday activities much more difficult. Kymlicka argues that most people are closely bound to the cultural community in which they were raised, and that people can be expected to want access to their own culture and to suffer when it is not available. He admits that members of minority cultures are entitled to leave their culture if they choose to do so. But this admission is consistent with his insistence that cultural membership is not something that they can fairly be asked to give up if they do not choose to do so.[20] In order to preserve their culture, national minorities seem to be entitled to pursue pseudo-separatist policies and to live in relative isolation from the rest of society (if that is what is plausibly required to maintain their cultural practices). And in Kymlicka's view, fairness towards national minorities would require support from the wider society.

This is not the place to discuss the extensive literature that Kymlicka's arguments in defense of "special rights" for cultural minorities has generated.[21] For our purposes, the question is whether his argument could be used to construct a consistent extension of Rawls' theory of justice that is capable of addressing at least some of the problems generated by cultural pluralism. Joseph Carens argues that this is not the case. He objects to Kymlicka's claim that cultural belonging should be treated as a Rawlsian social primary good.[22] As we have seen, the distribution of social primary goods is regulated in Rawls' theory by the two principles of justice, which have a lexical ordering. If we consider adding cultural belonging to Rawls' list of social primary goods we would have to establish whether this is the kind of good that should be distributed according to the first principle or according to the second principle. Moreover, Carens also points out that we cannot assume that the distribution of the good of cultural belonging will not affect the distribution of Rawls' official social primary goods. So we face the additional theoretical difficulty of establishing priorities between securing the good of cultural belonging and, say, securing freedom of expression, or freedom of movement, or opportunity to access desirable social positions. Carens' objections might be taken merely to suggest that Kymlicka's argument is incomplete and that he could overcome the objections simply by answering the questions just posed. But in my view, the problem with Kymlicka's suggestion is not so easily solvable. If we try to settle the question of what kind of good cultural belonging is, we should conclude that cultural belonging is simply not the kind of good that major social institutions can actually distribute in the way that they can distribute liberties, opportunities, and economic resources. In my view, the complexity and variability of cultural phenomena, and the fact that cultural communities are often intermingled and share the same territory, prevents us from treating cultural belonging as a good on a par with Rawls' official social primary goods.

Jeremy Waldron has raised a related challenge to Kymlicka's argument for the significance of cultural belonging in people's pursuit of their conceptions of the good.[23] Waldron argues against Kymlicka's central claim that human beings *need* a stable cultural framework—the cultural framework in which they were raised—in order to develop and pursue their conception of the good.[24] Against that idea, he points to the viability of adopting a cosmopolitan approach towards culture:

> The cosmopolitan may live all his life in one city and maintain the same citizenship throughout. But he refuses to think of himself as defined by his location or his ancestry or his citizenship or his language. Though he may live in San Francisco and be of Irish ancestry, he does not take his identity to be compromised when he learns Spanish, eats Chinese, wears clothes made in Korea, listens to arias by Verdi sung by a Maori princess on Japanese equipment, follows Ukrainian politics, and practices Buddhist meditation techniques. He is a creature of modernity, conscious of living in a mixed-up world and having a mixed-up self.[25]

The cosmopolitan approach to culture acknowledges that people make use of 'cultural materials' when deciding about how to live meaningful lives. But instead of focusing on reproducing the culture of one's ancestors, the cosmopolitan will be happy to eat different foods, learn foreign languages, or adopt a philosophical outlook that comes from very distant lands. This possibility challenges the idea that people need just one single, coherent cultural structure if they are to be able to have a meaningful life. In particular, it challenges the idea that people need access to the culture of the group in which they were raised, thus undermining the claim that cultural belonging should be regarded as a basic social good. As we have seen, Kymlicka argues that it is only by having a coherent, rich, and secure cultural structure that people can become sufficiently aware of the worthwhile options available to them. But, for Waldron, such worthwhile options do not need to proceed from only one cultural source. Rather, they may be patched together from fragments belonging to the myriad of different cultural sources that are available in contemporary societies. Waldron claims that cosmopolitan lifestyles that consciously celebrate the mix of cultural materials are perfectly viable, and they can be as fulfilling as more traditional lifestyles. Moreover, according to Waldron, this kind of cosmopolitan alternative is available not only to those who immigrate or travel frequently, but to anybody who enjoys exploring the kaleidoscope of cultural materials that are present in contemporary societies. Waldron's cosmopolitan is someone who refuses to identify herself with her location, ancestry, citizenship, or mother tongue. She is aware of cultural mixing and openly endorses this mix. If it is possible for people to find this sort of cosmopolitan lifestyle satisfactory, then, Waldron argues, a central premise in Kymlicka's argument is called into question: the premise that the meaning, integrity, and coherence of an individual's life depends on immersion in the shared culture of one single community to which a person belongs.

Waldron also thinks that there tends to be a false premise in approaches that tie individual self-fulfillment to a secure cultural context, because such approaches often rely on rather distorted, static, and purist pictures of particular cultures. But, like all living phenomena, cultures are constantly changing. Moreover, there has never been anything like the culture of a human group that has been completely isolated from the influence of others.[26] Now it is true that some defenders of cultural preservation may work with a picture of a flourishing culture frozen in the past. But this particular objection does not really work against Kymlicka's view, since Kymlicka does not argue in favor of efforts to maintain the 'purity' of minority cultures. Kymlicka's concern is only to prevent the majority culture from exercising irresistible pressures on minority cultures. The measures that Kymlicka endorses are not designed to prevent cultural change. Rather, they simply aim to give national minorities some political control of the ways in which that change will occur. Nevertheless, Waldron tends to see attempts to preserve or protect the culture of groups as rowing against the waves, and the desire to share one's life primarily with members of one's culture, separated from the rest of society, as a sign of an artificial attitude. In fact, he provocatively compares this desire with the desire to live in Disneyland.[27]

Waldron contrasts two models for conceptualizing an individual's cultural identity in a multicultural society. According to the first model, the one person/one culture model, each person builds her own identity by relying on the unique and relatively homogeneous culture of the group to which she belongs. According to the second model, the one person/many fragments model, each person builds her identity by using materials from the wider society in which she lives. This second model implies that each person's sense of identity inevitably includes a multiplicity of heterogeneous cultural fragments that superpose and overlap, even if there may be one culture with predominant influence. At least in some of his writings Kymlicka seems to operate with the model of one person/one culture, because he associates culture very closely with language, and he thinks of culture as institutionally embodied in government, schools, media, and so on.[28] In response to Waldron's objections, Kymlicka admits that some exceptional people are capable of 'switching' or moving between cultures and of constructing identities out of a mix of cultural materials. Kymlicka points out that many people who immigrate can integrate and function relatively well in their new countries, leading good lives there. But many others find it extremely difficult to adjust to their new environment, and decide to return home. And still others never want to leave in the first place. So the fact that some individuals who immigrate successfully manage to live lives moving across cultures does very little to prove, for Kymlicka, that most people are not deeply connected to their own culture, or that moving to another culture is not an extremely costly process in most cases. Kymlicka rightly notes that the costs can be expected to vary with age, and in proportion to the degree of similarity between the languages and histories of the two cultures. I would add that individual temperament, personal interests, and the extent to which institutions and individual citizens are welcoming of newcomers also play a role in the successful integration of immigrants.

In opposition to Waldron, Kymlicka denies that an Irish American who lives in San Francisco is genuinely living in a kaleidoscope of cultures, or moving between cultures, simply by virtue of eating Chinese food, listening to operas, or practicing Buddhist meditation. Kymlicka would describe this person as someone who is merely enjoying the opportunities available in the anglophone culture of the United States. It seems that to move between cultures in Kymlicka's sense one would have to move to and settle in a territory that is controlled by a different nation: a place where there is a wide network of social institutions that embody the culture of a nation that is foreign. I myself find Kymlicka's conceptualization of cultural phenomena, and its focus only on the culture embodied in major social institutions, too tidy. It may be true that one or two cultures predominate in the government, schools, or mass media in any given contemporary multicultural society. But there are many other important social institutions that operate according to the norms of a wide range of different cultures. For example, there are families, markets, small media, and schools (depending on what the law of the country allows) that operate on the basis of minority cultures. The fact that a number of cultural communities with different cultural practices coexist within a single territory affects the shared public life of citizens and the life prospects and opportunities that members of those different groups have. Kymlicka's picture fails to give due attention to the extent to which individuals actually can incorporate very heterogeneous cultural materials and hold a variety of cultural affiliations and identifications at the same time. It underestimates the extent to which many people are capable of active bilingualism, ignoring, for example, the situation of those who grow up in families with members of different ethnocultural backgrounds, the situation of the children of immigrants who have to navigate significantly different cultural norms at home and at school, or the situation of the increasing number of people whose professional lives require a good deal of travel to foreign countries. Kymlicka is aware of the existence of these phenomena, but his theory of cultural membership fails to give them sufficient importance, assuming they are less common, or perhaps less significant, than they actually are.

These criticisms of Kymlicka should not be taken to indicate that I agree entirely with Waldron. In fact, Waldron's approach seems to err in the opposite direction. By talking about the undeniable fact of cultural mixing, he seems to underemphasize the fact that some cultural practices do predominate in one society, even if they are not 'pure' but are a mix of cultural practices. His remarks also make it seem that appropriation of new cultural materials is always easy. Perhaps it *is* easy to travel and to find one's way around in other countries and cultures if one speaks English, has enough money, and has the kind of passport that opens the doors at national borders. The world may therefore present a much more open appearance to those, like Waldron, who can do so. Waldron also draws a picture according to which we have a variety of cultures available to us and we can freely choose to incorporate whatever fragments strike our fancy. This may be the case with some cultural materials, such as food, music, or clothing. But this should not blind us to the fact that languages and prevalent cultural norms can act as significant barriers to people's prospects for successful integration into central social and political institutions, and that learning new languages and norms can sometimes be very hard. Waldron rejects policies supporting the preservation of the culture of national minorities, but he does not seem to appreciate the human costs involved in their disappearance.[29] To my knowledge he does not endorse policies especially designed to facilitate the successful integration of national minorities or immigrants; nor does he seem to acknowledge the sense of cultural loss that many immigrants experience.

Cultural Pluralism and Educational Policies

I have contrasted the ways in which Kymlicka and Waldron conceptualize the multicultural character of society in order to shed light on the question of how to extend Rawls' simplified model of a pluralist society. Kymlicka rightly reminds us that some cultural practices do predominate in society, and that political communities unavoidably make decisions that affect the prospects of cultural reproduction of majority and minority groups. Waldron rightly reminds us that people have the capacity to appropriate new cultural materials and learn from other cultural groups, without necessarily feeling that their identity is threatened or that their prospects for a good life are doomed. Individuals and groups can change their ways of doing things in more or less radical ways, either abruptly or over a long period of time. Not all members of society share the same ways of doing things, but they will inevitably find themselves sharing many social spaces: at work, at school, in the market, in political parties, and in innumerable other social venues. Given that some cultural practices will predominate in the social institutions of a particular society, different groups of citizens will be positioned in better or worse ways to take advantage of the liberties and opportunities that the society makes available. Now, assuming that the principles of justice can provide us with good guidelines to assess the justice of the basic structure, a central question is the following: how might a society be able to satisfy the two principles under conditions of pervasive cultural pluralism?

One route towards an answer to this question would be to try to think about the kinds of laws that impartial legislators who endorse the principles of justice would select if they knew the particular circumstances of their society. We can imagine that these legislators are making decisions about policies and have some information about the cultural makeup of their society, but do not know whether they themselves belong to the national majority, or to a national minority, or to an immigrant group. We can then try to figure out which policies, given the circumstances, would better protect the interests of everyone, particularly those of the least-advantaged individuals. One problem with this thought experiment is that we have to consider not only the interests of members of minority groups who are deeply concerned with preserving their cultural practices, but also the interests of individual members of these groups who may be dissidents or may have very little power within their group. Because of complications like these, quite often there may be no clear or simple answer regarding the best policy, even if people are trying to be impartial and to make an adequate assessment of the benefits and burdens generated by the alternative policies. But we may nevertheless find a range of reasonable policies that a society might adopt to improve the situation of those members whose life prospects are the worst, due to cultural differences as well as to past and present injustices affecting cultural minorities. Of course the particular policies that are appropriate responses to the situation of cultural minorities will depend to a great extent on the particular nature of the relevant injustices. But I do not want to discuss any particular policy in much detail here, since my main concern is at a higher level: to argue that a Rawlsian understanding of social justice should be combined with policies that are designed to accommodate the legitimate claims of members of cultural minorities. I will argue that, if one accepts Rawls' principles of justice, one should also support policies designed to facilitate the voluntary integration of members of cultural minorities into major social institutions, as well as to accommodate their reasonable demands to maintain some cultural practices and pass them on to new generations.

In my view, the best place to introduce considerations of cultural pluralism is at the level of *application* of the theory. If we take Rawls' principles seriously, then we should endorse at least some policies of accommodation of cultural differences in order to facilitate the integration of members of minority cultures and in that way secure their opportunities and access to resources. For such policies of accommodation to be effective, a willingness to adapt to a pluralist cultural environment should work in both directions. That is, both members of the majority culture and members of the minority cultures should be willing to find just ways of living and doing things together. This implies not only that citizens should support the state adopting policies of accommodation, but also that they make an effort to cooperate with others who may have very different cultural backgrounds.[30] However, there are limits on the degree to which the state can produce this kind of mutual accommodation if the members of society are not willing to do their part. There is a wide range of eligible policies facilitating the voluntary integration of minority groups in shared public spaces. I will mention some of them in what follows. But respect for freedom of association requires that citizens should be free to choose who to marry, with whom to make friends, or with whom to share other private social activities. So there are significant and obvious limits to the state's legitimate power to push for integration.[31]

We have seen that Rawls' model of a just society does not take into account the significance of the fact of cultural pluralism, nor do his views of the kinds of attitudes and qualities of reasonable citizens that support the stability of just institutions. But cultural differences do have a pervasive impact on shared public life, as well as on the individual life prospects of citizens. We have discussed some of the difficulties of attempts to incorporate cultural belonging at the foundational level of Rawls' theory. The nature of cultural phenomena suggests that cultural belonging is not a good that can be distributed by the institutions of the basic structure in accordance with the principles of justice. And the variability of human capacities to adjust to cultural change suggests that it need not play the role in individuals' pursuit of a good life that Kymlicka claims it plays. Still, cultural background has an impact on many central issues of justice. Although cultural background does not affect the basic rights and liberties of citizens protected by law, it certainly has a profound impact on the kinds of opportunities different groups have available, including their prospects of making a decent income.[32]

One might be able to use the requirements of the second principle of justice as a general justification for policies that facilitate the voluntary integration of cultural minorities. We can call these policies 'multicultural,' provided we keep in mind that there are many very different proposals that are currently being defended under the banner of multiculturalism, and that not all these policies are compatible with the ones advocated in this chapter.[33] Moreover, I think that Rawls' principles of justice do not require state support for the pseudo-separatist projects of some minority groups, given that the most likely consequence of such projects will be the marginalization of the members of those groups from the rest of society, and the denial of opportunities to their children.[34] This would involve violating the second principle of justice. Of course, adult citizens who belong to cultural minorities should be free to maintain their cultural practices and teach their children he same. But children should also be taught about the prevalent cultural practices in the wider society, so that they have a real opportunity to choose how to live their lives when they become adults.

In order to facilitate the integration of cultural minorities, a number of multicultural educational policies should be adopted, making social institutions more welcoming to different cultural groups, and encouraging positive attitudes towards cultural pluralism.[35] First of all, the integration of cultural minorities goes hand in hand with a multicultural curriculum, both in public and private schools. Such a curriculum will acknowledge the contribution of cultural minorities to the common culture of the country, as well as their role in the history of the country. As I argued in chapter 7, the teaching of history should not ignore or misrepresent past injustices in order to encourage patriotic identification. Rather, it should try to make students more aware of what actually happened, and of the variety of points of view and the complexity involved in the study of the past. Even though some critics of multiculturalism find this approach "too divisive," members of minority groups will feel that their points of view are respected only by a more honest approach to the past that acknowledges their grievances.[36] This need not involve retelling history exclusively from the point of view of a minority group, since there are historical facts and historical records to be taken into account. Moreover, reasonable disputes in the interpretation of these facts should be made explicit as well.

Schools should adjust their rules so as to make students of different cultural backgrounds feel as welcome and as comfortable as possible. In particular, this will require policies of accommodation for religious holidays, dress codes, and types of food served in cafeterias, among other things. It will also include implementing school behavior codes that discourage racism and the expression of ethnic insults. But such institutional measures are not sufficient if students do not also learn something substantial about the cultures and traditions of different groups or if they fail to have a positive attitudes towards cultural diversity. It is particularly important that children learn to appreciate the cultural practices of their fellow students. On many occasions, hostility and distrust towards members of cultural minorities, whether national minorities or recent immigrants, is the result of serious ignorance about other groups' values and ways of life. Students should be encouraged to have a more open attitude towards their classmates and they should be willing to learn about them and interact with them. A very likely result of this sort of encouragement would be an appreciation of the rich diversity even among members of the same cultural group, and a more nuanced view about their ways of life.

Policies of bilingual education and foreign language programs are more controversial. I myself do not see much sense in the controversies over bilingual education, which seem to be caused by increased hostility towards immigrants and fear that they will 'take over.' At the very least, schools should offer classes for children (and adults) who have recently immigrated and need to learn the predominant language if they are to succeed in their new home. Depending on facts about numbers and territorial concentration, the ideal of integration also favors setting up extensive voluntary bilingual programs in primary and secondary school. If a country has a sizeable and territorially concentrated linguistic minority, schools should make it possible for minority children to get instruction in the language spoken by the majority, but also to choose to get additional instruction in their mother tongue. And children from the cultural majority should have the opportunity to choose to learn some of the languages spoken by minority groups as well. Although I am not an expert in socio-linguistics, some fierce opponents of bilingual education seem to me to underestimate the capacity of children to learn more than one language at a young age. Public support for bilingual education sends a very powerful message that the state does not belong only to the cultural majority but also to the cultural minority groups. It also, quite plausibly, would have significant integrative effects. The success of such programs would allow children to become proficient in two languages, increasing their opportunities in the future as well as their capacities to communicate with fellow citizens. Of course, whether I am right or not depends on empirical issues that are beyond my particular expertise.[37]

The policies of multicultural education that I have just discussed aim to facilitate the integration of cultural minorities and their participation in major social institutions, so that the children in these groups can better enjoy the liberties, opportunities, and material resources available in society. Processes of integration require efforts by members of both the majority and minority cultures to cooperate with fellow citizens on fair terms. The fact that such personal efforts are required supports the idea that schools should encourage children and adolescents to learn more about the cultures of fellow citizens. But mere knowledge is not enough. They must also learn to be open to changing their ways of doing things—sometimes a little, sometimes a lot—in order to accommodate the reasonable demands of others. Teaching children how to find reasonable compromises is a central task of civic education under conditions of deep cultural diversity.

9   Concluding Remarks

In this book I have offered an interpretation of John Rawls' theory of justice as fairness and of the role that educational institutions have—or should have—in the theory. As part of that effort I have tried to clarify his very complex model of a just society and his account of reasonable citizenship. This paved the way for a clearer discussion of the contribution that families and schools can make to sustain, or to create, a just society of the kind defended by Rawls by educating reasonable citizens. One valuable aspect of Rawls' theory is that it takes justice to be a property of the set of major social and political institutions of society, working together as a system. As we saw in chapter 4, this implies that it would be a mistake to try to apply the principles of justice directly to the functioning of one social institution alone, such as the family or the educational system. This theory is not meant to answer the question of what just families are like, or what just schools are like. Rather, it is meant to provide a model of a just society as a whole. Partly with this kind of institutional interdependence in mind, I argued that the tasks of families and schools should complement each other: schools cannot provide the kind of emotional and moral support that families give (in well-functioning families), and families cannot provide the diverse and rule-structured environment of schools that encourages the development of capacities for reasonability (again, in well-functioning schools). But institutional dependence does not mean that the failures of schools or families can always be blamed on external factors. Rawls' theory places certain requirements on how these institutions should function: there are certain threshold capacities that these institutions must help cultivate if they are to play their role within the overall system.

There is another corollary of Rawls' systematic approach that is worth stressing, even if it might seem obvious to many readers: schools' contribution to achieving justice in society is significant but it is unavoidably limited, and cannot be separated from the contribution that other sectors of society must make. I would not like to give the misleading impression that I hold the main solution to most social evils to be better education provided by schools. I do not think that *all* that is needed to improve societies is that schools manage to educate children in the right way, that is, to teach them to appreciate their rights and the rights of others, to engage with others on reasonable terms, and to develop the set of skills and capacities that will enable them to have a good life in the future. Nor do I want to suggest that schools or teachers are to blame when children finish school having failed to learn these things. We live under social institutions that send out a huge array of conflicting messages and that encourage students to think of themselves, their life prospects, their fellows, and their society in a wide variety of potentially incompatible ways. Even if schools do their part in teaching the valuable political ideals of fairness and respect for freedom and equality, these messages may not have sufficient impact when they are too starkly at odds with what children and adolescents are picking up in other parts of their lives. A good number of the reforms that would make schools more effective at encouraging good citizenship and a mature sense of justice lie outside of schools themselves. Among the most urgent of these reforms include those aimed at the reduction of poverty and violence, the improvement of housing, and the provision of better access to health care.

The interpretation of the theory of justice offered in this book has taken into account the changes that Rawls introduced in his theory after his political turn. This required looking at Rawls' early work in a selective way, leaving aside those aspects of his early theory that are in conflict with the political restrictions on justification. What is most significant about the political turn is the attempt to demonstrate that the principles of justice can be acceptable to reasonable citizens who hold a variety of comprehensive doctrines and conceptions of the good life. Rawls argues that the principles of justice that regulate the basic structure could be at the focus of an 'overlapping consensus' of reasonable citizens. He also recommends that public debates about the constitution and about matters of basic justice should be conducted in terms of 'public reasons.' That is, such debates should avoid appeal to comprehensive doctrines that not all citizens share. But because this restriction applies only at the very high level of constitutional reform and matters of basic justice, it is not very clear what follows if one is trying to provide guidelines for educational policy, or to explain the kinds of things that schools are required or allowed to do to support social justice. According to the interpretation that I defended in this book, Rawls provides some general prescriptions for the education of citizens, but he is concerned that his prescriptions satisfy the general guidelines of political argumentation. This is why he refuses to appeal to ideals such as personal autonomy or individuality as part of the required contents of civic education: these ideals are not shared by all reasonable citizens. But this is very different from saying that the political justification of policies requires actual consensus among the citizens of real societies. 'Overlapping consensus' is a technical notion in Rawls' theory, and the possibility of achieving overlapping consensus, as Rawls understands it, does not require reaching consensus on actual policies. Similar remarks can be made about the ideal of public reason: it is not an ideal that makes sense to apply to discussions at

Parents/Teachers Association meetings, or to class debates. It is certainly valuable if schools encourage students to try to find reasons that other people can accept as relevant. This can be seen as part of the general task of cultivating a general civil disposition to engage in dialogue in respectful terms. But this is different from Rawls' recommendation that considerations that appeal to comprehensive doctrines about the good should be avoided in public debates concerning constitutional essentials and matters of basic justice. Such debates touch on the functioning of the basic structure of society, and it is important that the principles that regulate this functioning could be acceptable to reasonable citizens. Debates in schools will not have this type of impact, and it would be inappropriate to transplant the requirements of public reason to this micro-level. In fact, as I argued in chapter 5, schools should make room for respectful exploration of a variety of conceptions of the good, since this is part of what is needed to cultivate reasonability and mutual understanding.

In the previous three chapters of the book I developed Rawls' theory in directions that he himself did not explore, but that are (I hope) consistent with his views. Of course I have to acknowledge the possibility that Rawls could have reached very different conclusions on the topics I discuss in these chapters. After all, his theory of international justice turned out to be very different from what theorists predicted. It might seem puzzling that a theory that is explicitly built on an ideal of free and equal citizens denies that the education of children should be guided by a comprehensive ideal of personal autonomy. But we should keep in mind how controversial such an ideal is bound to be. There are disagreements not only about the value of ideals of personal autonomy as part of a conception of the good life, but, also, among those who defend autonomy as an ideal, about how to characterize the ideal itself. If we try to find common ground among the proponents of autonomy, I suspect that we are quite likely to be left with only a very minimalist account that has lost much of what made the idea attractive and distinctive to its proponents in the first place. Of course one might always try to defend a detailed and robust notion of personal autonomy and show that most children will be unable to find a good life unless they manage to achieve such autonomy. But that would be to give up many of Rawls' plausible premises: premises that I have taken as starting point in this book. It seems to me that the idea of freedom as non-domination provides a clearer alternative to any conception of autonomy. And, since there is much more agreement that domination is an evil than that autonomy is a good, appeal to non-domination has the advantage of fitting better with the requirements of political justification.

I also extend Rawls' theory somewhat when addressing questions about the value of patriotic or nationalist feelings, and whether they should be cultivated in schools. These questions are hard to answer within the theory as Rawls presents it. This is because his model of a just society involves a number of simplifications that allow him to deal with very complex social phenomena. For similar reasons his model of a just international order involves a number of simplifications as well: it has us imagine societies that are self-contained, which makes mass immigration 'not a problem' within the theory. My strategy, in the face of these kinds of theoretical simplifications, has been to use the principles of justice as guidelines to assess the level of justice in real, multicultural, societies and to ask what kind of educational policies would support the fulfillment of the principles. It is in applying the theory in this way that we can take into account the complexity of these societies and the fact that citizens may have a variety of political identifications. And if we do so, I believe that we should not find it persuasive that patriotic or nationalist feelings are instrumental to social justice (much less to international justice). We would do better to focus on teaching core values of political justice and a range of political virtues. Not only would this avoid the liabilities of patriotic civic education, but it might be one of the most useful ways to encourage mutual understanding among members of societies with different national and cultural affiliations.

Notes

Chapter 1

1 See Parry (1999); for a sample of articles that discuss the educational views of influential political philosophers see Rorty (1998).
2 For a survey of debates about citizenship, see Kymlicka and Norman (1994); Costa (2009a). On citizenship and education, see Callan (2004).
3 See McDonough and Feinberg (2003).
4 See, among others Arneson and Shapiro (1996); Burtt (1996); Galeotti (1996); Galston (1995); Galston (2002), pp. 93–109; Gutmann (1993); Gutmann (1995); Laborde (2008); Macedo (1995).
5 See Feinberg (2003); Halstead (2003); MacMullen (2007); Spinner-Halev (2000).
6 See Norman (1998). This paragraph owes much to Daniels' assessment of the impact of Rawls' early works. See Daniels (1989a), pp. xxxi–liv.
7 Some books that rely heavily on Rawls' work are: Strike (1982); Strike (1989); Callan (1997); Clayton (2006); Macedo (2000); Tomasi (2001).
8 For example, John Tomasi's discussion of education is grounded in Rawls' work, but a careful reading reveals that Tomasi does not really endorse the redistributive implications of Rawls' theory. Rather, he thinks that the theory should make more room for personal responsibility. See Tomasi (2001), pp. 108–25. And Eamonn Callan rejects Rawls' method of political justification and endorses a liberal perfectionist approach grounded on the value of personal autonomy. See Callan (1997), pp. 12–42.
9 Rawls (1996); Rawls (1999a); Rawls (2001).
10 The idea that the family is the first school of justice is taken from Okin (1989), pp. 17–24.
11 See Pettit (1999).

Chapter 2

1 See Rawls (1999a), pp. 3–10; Rawls (1996), pp. 257–88.
2 Rawls (1996), p. 258.
3 Rawls (1999a), pp. 47–48.
4 Rawls (1996), p. 269.
5 This is true even for societies that allow forms of home schooling, in which parents or legal tutors assume the responsibility for providing formal instruction to their children. Of course, there is a prior question as to whether these ways of educating children are consistent with the promotion of social justice and good citizenship. One might also argue that the health care system should be considered to be a part of the basic structure. For the sake of simplicity, Rawls does

not take the health care system into account in his theory, but he does think that guaranteed access to health care is a central institutional feature of a just society. See Rawls (1999b), p. 50.

6 See Young (2006). Young agrees with Rawls' insight regarding the significance of the basic structure, but she claims that there are certain forms of structural injustice that Rawls' theory fails to illuminate. For criticisms of the idea that the principles that apply to the basic structure should be regarded as different from the principles that apply directly to individual behavior, see Cohen (2000), pp. 134–47 and Murphy (1999).

7 Mandle (2000), p. 29.

8 Some critics of Rawls challenge this assumption, claiming that there is a global basic structure and global institutions that have functions that are very similar to those of their domestic counterparts. Rawls' own view is that there are significant asymmetries between domestic and global institutions, and that the set of global institutions does not amount to something sufficiently similar to the domestic basic structure for the same theory to apply to both.

9 Rawls (2001), p. 11.

10 It is a common mistake to try to apply Rawls' principles of justice as criteria for just distributions of resources in arbitrary contexts, without taking into account the type of institutional structure at stake. For example, some have tried to use Rawls' difference principle to decide about the distribution of medical resources at micro levels. Unsurprisingly, this results in highly counterintuitive policy recommendations. Using this approach, one might easily conclude that priority should be given to those in intensive care units because they are the worst off. But this is clearly a misapplication of the theory.

11 Rawls' principles of international justice are the following (1999b, p. 37):

1. Peoples are free and independent, and their freedom and independence are to be respected by other peoples.
2. Peoples are to observe treaties and undertakings.
3. Peoples are equal and are parties to the agreements that bind them.
4. Peoples are to observe a duty of non-intervention.
5. Peoples have the right to self-defense but no right to instigate war for reasons other than self-defense.
6. Peoples are to honor human rights.
7. Peoples are to observe certain specified restrictions in the conduct of war.
8. Peoples have a duty to assist other peoples living under unfavorable conditions that prevent their having a just or decent political and social regime.

12 For an extended discussion see Sangiovanni (2008).

13 In contrast, a theory of justice for the local level or for the international order needs to be developed against a background of other institutional arrangements, and other shared normative ideals.

14 Rawls (1996), pp. 11–15.

15 Rawls (1996), pp. 11–15.

16 Rawls (1996), pp. 16–17.

17 Rawls (1996), pp. 18–20.

18 This account of the idea of citizens as free and equal has been criticized on a number of grounds. To avoid some misunderstandings, it is important to make clear that Rawls does not deny the rights of individuals with serious mental disabilities who do not seem capable of coming up to the required threshold. Rawls' model idealizes human beings as fully cooperating members of society during the whole course of their lives. And his principles of justice are developed with an eye to the regulation of the relationships of citizens understood in this way. But it

does not follow that those who do not satisfy the threshold should not count as citizens with valid claims. Rather, it only follows that their interests are considered at a further stage of the theory. For an extension of Rawls' theory of justice to meet the interests of seriously mentally disabled citizens see Richardson (2006).

19 Rawls (1999a), p. 119.
20 Rawls (1999c), pp. 362–63.
21 One possible additional good that Rawls discusses is leisure time, defined as the residual time that someone has after working. Including this good might help us make more precise interpersonal comparisons between different groups of people than if we used income alone. Two groups' situations might seem very different if we look only at their income, but they may be roughly equivalent if people in one of them earn twice as much as those in the other but also work twice as many hours. A further complication, however, is that not all socially useful work receives direct monetary compensation. In particular, this is true of much of the work that women are socially expected to do, such as caring for children, as well as any disabled or sick members of the family. So we cannot simply assume that those who do not engage in paid work have more of the good of leisure.
22 Rawls (1999d), p. 491.
23 Rawls (1996), p. 5. I examine the details of this principle and the next in the following section, and also in chapter 6.
24 Rawls (1996), p. 6.
25 Barry (1995), p. 894.
26 See the discussion in Pogge (2007), pp. 126–33.
27 H.L.A. Hart has pointed out that there was a tension in the 1971 version of *A Theory of Justice* between some passages that referred to liberty in general terms and some that referred to the basic liberties of citizens. Rawls acknowledged this criticism and revised his theory accordingly, focusing only on the distribution of basic liberties. See Hart (1989); Rawls (1996), pp. 289–371.
28 Rawls (1996), p. 291. The following explanation of the activities covered by each basic liberty borrows heavily from Freeman (2007), pp. 44–59. For an assessment of the list see Martin (1985), pp. 45–61; Nickel (1993–94).
29 Rawls (1996), pp. 292–93.
30 Rawls (1996), p. 325.
31 Freeman (2007), pp. 48–49.
32 Rawls (1999a), pp. 178–79.
33 This change was motivated by Norman Daniels' criticisms. See Daniels (1989b).
34 I return to this principle in chapters 4 and 6.
35 Rawls (1999a), p. 63.
36 Mason (2006), pp. 72–73.
37 Susan Moller Okin points out that one effect of the structure of the labor market is that many jobs and positions, including highly desirable ones, are difficult or impossible to combine with childcare responsibilities that tend to fall disproportionately on women. See Okin (1989). I will examine some of Okin's interesting criticisms of Rawls' theory of justice in chapter 4.
38 The way of understanding the principle of fair equality of opportunity that lies behind Rawls' pessimism here is very demanding; it requires that access to desirable social positions not depend at all on the social background in which someone is raised. A more moderate interpretation would require only that there be policies designed to reduce the impact of social background, not that it have no effects at all on someone's life prospects. See Daniels (2003) and Freeman (2007), pp. 86–98; for a moderate interpretation.
39 For an examination of these kinds of objections see Schaller (1998).

40 In *Political Liberalism*, Rawls mentions that his principles of justice should be supplemented by a guaranteed social minimum, understood as the minimum resources required for citizens to meet their basic needs. See Rawls (1996), p. 7. Walter Schaller explains the reason for this additional requirement in the following way: even if the difference principle ensures that the lifetime expectations of the least advantaged group are as high as possible, the actual income that some individual may earn may fall below what is necessary for satisfying her or her family's needs. This may be the result of illness, unemployment, loss of partner, or other factors. See Schaller (1998). For a radical interpretation of the difference principle as the basis for an unconditional basic income see Van Parijs (2003).

41 See Rawls (2001), pp. 135–140.

Chapter 3

1 See Rawls (1996), p. 35.

2 I do not mean to suggest that children inevitably inherit their parents' comprehensive doctrines. The point is only that each new generation will enter active political life with a variety of strong and potentially conflicting views about the good life.

3 See Rawls (2001), pp. 196–97.

4 See Rawls (1999a), pp. 397–449. It may be worth mentioning that Rawls' story lays equal emphasis on the roles of moral feelings and of moral reasoning. This undercuts some criticisms he has received, which claim that he endorses a Kantian account of the self as free from ties, feelings, and attachments: a disembodied self. These criticisms extrapolate unfairly from Rawls' characterization of the original position, and completely ignore Rawls' account of moral development. See Sandel (1998).

5 See Piaget (1932); Kohlberg (1984). Kohlberg's theory of moral development has received a number of criticisms. The most influential of these was Carol Gilligan's, who claimed that Kohlberg's theory failed to take into account moral thinking centered on the activity of care. See Gilligan (1982). It is worth emphasizing that methodological disputes about Piaget, Kohlberg, or Gilligan's work do not directly touch Rawls' account of moral development, because his account is not defended as a scientific theory of human psychology.

6 See chapters 4 and 7 for further discussion of Rawls' account of moral development.

7 For a more detailed discussion of Rawls' account of moral development see Brennan and Noggle (2000).

8 For a detailed discussion of mistaken interpretations that rely on actual consensus see Kaufman (2006).

9 Rawls (1996), p. 59. I have edited and formatted Rawls here to make the three conditions more easily distinguishable.

10 See Barry (1995); Callan (1997), pp. 25–36; Wenar (1995).

11 Wenar argues against the idea that all reasonable citizens will accept the burdens of judgment, using official documents of the Catholic church as an example. One problem with his argument is that he assumes that the content of comprehensive doctrines is well defined and fixed. But official doctrines do not necessarily reflect the position of reasonable adherents of a particular faith. The same doctrine may be held in a reasonable or in an unreasonable way, and there are a number of reasonable disagreements among adherents to a particular faith. See Krasnoff (1998).

12 See Daniels (1996), p. 157.

13 Rawls (1996), p. 227.

14 Rawls (1996), pp. 228–29.
15 See Rawls (1996) pp. 199–200; Rawls (2001), pp. 156–57.

Chapter 4

1 For criticisms of policies based on these assumptions see Burtt (2002); Young (1994).
2 About the diversity of family forms and values of families see Halstead (1999).
3 Macleod (2002), pp. 213–14.
4 Rawls (1999a), chapter 8.
5 For some early feminist criticisms of Rawls see English (1977); Kearns (1983); Okin (1989). For a survey of more recent feminist criticisms see Nussbaum (2003). Rawls briefly responds to some of this criticisms in Rawls (1999b), pp. 156–64; Rawls (2001), pp. 162–68.
6 In support of this interpretation of the claim that the principles of justice do not apply directly to the family, see Lloyd (1995), pp. 1326–29. In contrast, Okin claims that the principles of justice should apply directly to the family. But, as I argue later, Okin's position depends on a reading of the requirements of fair equality of opportunity and the difference principle that, while independently plausible, goes well beyond Rawls' texts. See Okin (1989); Okin (2004).
7 I would favor a policy of paying all families with children a certain fixed amount for the work of child care. One might object that it is not accurate to call domestic tasks and child care "unpaid work," since in a number of countries family income is considered common property. However, it is still generally the case that the adult who has paid work has direct control of the use of the resulting income (at least until divorce). Moreover, many countries do not treat family income in this way. And in many places the law does not secure adequate levels of alimony in case of divorce.
8 The fact that there are sometimes very significant exit costs to a marriage does not make the relationship between adults any less voluntary. Moreover, the cost of exiting an association can be significant as well. For example, think of a catholic priest or nun who decides to leave his or her position.
9 Rawls (2001), p. 162.
10 For an exploration of alternative arrangements for the rearing and education of children within a general Rawlsian framework see Munoz-Dardé (1998); Munoz-Dardé (1999).
11 I will have more to say about the Rawlsian account of moral development in chapter 7, which addresses the role of patriotic sentiments in what Rawls calls "the morality of association" and "the morality of principle."
12 See Okin (1989). This argument was first briefly stated in Kearns (1983).
13 Okin's focus on families formed by heterosexual couples has been challenged in Kymlicka (1991). In a later paper, Okin argues that gay and lesbian families tend to be fairer in their division of domestic labor, perhaps because they are less influenced by existing cultural norms. See Okin (1996). In what follows, I use the terms 'husbands' and 'wives' for the sake of simplicity, but the claims are also meant to apply to the male and female members of unmarried heterosexual couples who are raising children.
14 Single-parent families may also perpetuate gender stereotypes by requiring that teenage daughters contribute to housework, but not teenage sons.
15 Okin (1994).
16 Similar remarks hold for the just internal organization of schools. For a general defense of the claim that different types of institutional structure are governed by different principles of justice see Sangiovanni (2008).

17 For a detailed discussion of the points of disagreement between Rawls and Okin see Baehr (1996).

18 Sharon Lloyd offers a number of insightful examples of ways in which the distribution of tasks inside the family may be unequal but acceptable on the basis of a conception of the good shared by the adult members of a family. One of her examples involves a couple that agrees that paid and childcare work will be done in a higher proportion by one of them, while the other devotes more time to finish with graduate training, which they expect will result in a higher family income in the future. Lloyd points out that it is important that the division of labor is perceived as fair by both adults, and that children know the reasons for the particular arrangement. See Lloyd (1995), pp. 1339–43.

19 See Rawls (2001), pp. 165–67.

20 Okin (1989), pp. 99–100.

21 See Okin (1994), p. 36. I thank Elizabeth Brake for pointing this out to me.

22 Joshua Cohen criticizes a number of Okin's claims along similar lines. See Cohen (1992).

23 Among other desirable policies we might mention maternity and paternity leave benefits, state-funded childcare, or mandated childcare benefits; requirements for business to have flexible working schedules; legislation that limits working hours and overtime; school hours that are as long as working hours; and state-funded summer camps. These and additional policies are necessary to support families headed by single parents, who face more difficulties than two-parent families to combine paid work and childcare.

24 For example, many academic couples who have children tend to divide their work along the lines advocated by Okin. This might of course be explained by their endorsement of liberal egalitarian ideals. But it also might have something to do with the fact that academic jobs tend to have more flexible working hours and allow professors to do some of their work, such as preparing for classes, at home.

25 Thanks to Colin Macleod for pressing this point.

26 See chapter 6.

27 See Lloyd (1995), p. 1335.

28 Okin and Reich (1999).

29 This issue is raised in Okin (1989), p. 95. For additional considerations regarding the definition and measurement of income see Bojer (2002), esp. 400–401.

30 See Fishkin (1983); Macleod (2002); Brighouse and Swift (2009b).

31 See Bojer (2000).

32 Just to give one example, expensive private schools might be allowed but heavily taxed, so that there are more funds to pay for the education of children who go to public schools. In this way, parental partiality could be channeled to work for the educational benefit of the worst-off children. In more general terms, expensive private schools could be justified if they resulted in maximizing the expectations of primary goods for the worst-off members of society.

33 See Walzer (1983), pp. 197–226.

34 See Barry (2003).

35 These remarks are inspired by points made by Anderson (2004); Satz (2007); Satz (2008); and Curren (1994). There is an active debate at present between these defenders of 'adequacy,' who favor some high (mostly non-comparative) threshold level of education, and defenders of 'equality,' who favor a more strictly egalitarian (comparative) per-student expenditure. For defenses of equality see Koski and Reich (2006); Brighouse and Swift (2008); Brighouse and Swift (2009a). The theoretical dispute between these two camps primarily concerns the question of whether or not, once the threshold has been achieved, justice allows inegalitarian expenditures in education. From a practical point of view, both groups

support reducing the current gap in expenditure of public funds per pupil in the United States (and in other countries as well), because the threshold that adequacy advocates have in mind is quite high, despite the very misleading connotations of the term. I will not attempt to settle this debate, since my main concern is to provide some guidelines regarding the ways in which families and schools should interact if they are to help satisfy the complex requirements of Rawls' principles of justice.

36 Brighouse (2000), pp. 121–22.
37 The question of what counts as a fair procedure for granting access to college and graduate schools is different from the question of what levels of income are fair for people who acquire an advanced degree. Some criticisms of meritocratic ideals are not really challenges to the allocation of relatively scarce social positions to those with more developed talents and skills, but are instead challenges to the enormous socioeconomic advantages that these positions carry with them.
38 These points are inspired by Elizabeth Anderson's objections to the applicability of a meritocratic principle of equality of opportunity to primary education. See Anderson (2004).
39 See Rawls (1999a), pp. 86–87.

Chapter 5

1 Rawls (2001), p. 146.
2 Rosenblum (1994); Callan (2004).
3 Kymlicka (2001), pp. 300–303.
4 Chambers and Kopstein (2001).
5 It is worth mentioning that there is another type of education for freedom that satisfies the requirements of public justification: education for non-domination. I argue, in the final section of chapter 6, that education for non-domination protects the basic interests of children, and can be justified in terms of public reasons.
6 See Kymlicka (1989b), pp. 884–85. Rawls also denies the feasibility of this type of neutrality in Rawls (1996), pp. 193–94.
7 This brief description of procedural neutrality is taken from Rawls (1996), p. 191. For a defense of this type of neutrality see Larmore (1987), pp. 53–59.
8 Rawls (1996), pp. 192–93.
9 The notion of public reason is grounded on the liberal principle of legitimacy, according to which "our exercise of political power is proper and hence justifiable only when it is exercised in accordance with a constitution the essentials of which all citizens may reasonably be expected to endorse in light of principles and ideals acceptable to them as reasonable and rational." Rawls (1996), p. 137. Of course, requiring that the essential elements of the constitution be acceptable to reasonable citizens does not answer all questions about the legitimate exercise of political authority, including the limits of the state's legitimate authority on issues regarding the education of children and adolescents. But it gives a presumption in favor of policies that can be justified in terms of shared public reasons.
10 See Weinstock (1999), p. 55.
11 See the excellent discussion by De Marneffe (2002), pp. 221–43. I agree with many of the points that De Marneffe makes, but my focus is different: how the notion of neutrality in education may be used within the Rawlsian framework that assumes the validity of the two principles of justice.
12 See MacIntyre (1990).
13 See McCabe (1998).
14 Rawls (2001), p. 156.

15 Rawls (2001), p. 157.

16 Other authors have pointed out that Rawls' theory of justice implies a more demanding account of civic education. See Callan (1997); Gutmann (1995); Mulhall (1998).

17 See Callan (1997), pp. 17–21; Gutmann (1995).

18 For an example of a comprehensive liberal theory that clearly goes beyond what a political liberal theory would recommend as regards children's education see Ackerman (1980), chapter 5. Ackerman recommends that teachers actively challenge conceptions of the good that children endorse.

19 I agree with many critics of Rawls' remarks on education for citizenship, who claim that the educational implications of his theory are much more substantial than he suggests. But these critics conclude that political liberalism is a form of comprehensive liberalism in disguise. In my view, the fact that Rawls' theory requires a more robust civic education does nothing to undermine his general strategy of political justification.

20 This sort of diversity is distinct from cultural diversity, which presents its own problems. I address these in chapter 8.

21 Strike (1993), p. 178.

22 Strike (1993), p. 178.

23 In the context of American public schools, liberal silence might also be the result of concerns about respecting the separation of church and state. Such concerns go as far as to make it difficult for music teachers to include devotional music in public performances, for fear of arousing the disapproval of their colleagues. In Argentina, by way of contrast, the Catholic church has had an enormous influence on educational policy. As a result, recent attempts to include a discussion of religious doctrines in public schools were interpreted as attempts to promote Catholicism. These proposals were consequently strongly opposed not only by those who defend the non-religious nature of public education, but also by representatives of other religious creeds.

24 See Callan (1997), pp. 26–39.

25 Callan (1997), p. 27. Callan claims that Rawls' theory is in fact comprehensive. This is because he interprets Rawls' requirement that citizens accept the burdens of judgment as involving an attitude of moral fallibilism or skepticism about one's conception of the good, which is incompatible with the way many people endorse their conceptions. But one does not need to be a fallibilist to be able to accept that others who disagree with one are still reasonable. See Garreta (2001).

26 McLaughlin (1995), pp. 248–50.

27 John Tomasi suggests that citizenship education should take into account the particular comprehensive doctrines of children (those they were taught at home) to help them integrate such doctrines with the political principles of justice. In his view this will allow them to "find ways to live lives of meaning and integrity given their own background and set of life experiences" (Tomasi (2001), p. 94). This might be plausible if it involves taking some doctrines as examples and examining ways of integrating them with political values. Perhaps there are some good novels that may serve this purpose. But Tomasi's suggestion is misguided if it involves asking children to talk about the personal meaning they attach to certain freedoms or political values, or raising any other questions concerning the congruence between justice and their own personal understandings of the good. There is no clear public benefit in asking students to explain their personal values to others; nor is it clear that students would benefit from being examined in this way.

28 I provide an account of these two virtues along Rawlsian lines in Costa (2004).

29 For an argument that social integration is crucial to fair equality of opportunity, see Anderson (2002).

Chapter 6

1 Rawls (1996), pp. 29–35; Rawls (2001), pp. 18–24.

2 See Rawls (1996), p. 291. The items on this list receive more explanation in chapter 2.

3 For discussions of Rawls' account of liberty and its compatibility with republican theories see Spitz (1993); Swift (1993); Pettit (1999), p. 50; Laden (2006); Larmore 2008, pp. 187–89.

4 MacCallum (1967).

5 Rawls (1999a), p. 177.

6 The only place where Rawls says anything about the freedom of collective agents is in his theory of international justice, in which he puts forward principles that require respect for the freedom of 'peoples' (which are reasonably just or decent countries). In this case, freedom amounts to self-government. See Rawls (1999b).

7 See Spitz (1993), p. 332; Pettit (1999), p. 50; Skinner (1983). However, Pettit (2008) is in many respects closer to Rawls' approach to the problem of liberty.

8 In his earlier work, Rawls makes use of a broadly Kantian notion of autonomy to justify the selection of the principles of justice. See Rawls (1999e). However, after the "political turn" he avoids appealing to this notion of moral autonomy because it is a comprehensive ideal that not all reasonable citizens share. But he continues to endorse the value of political autonomy understood as "the legal independence and assured integrity of citizens and their sharing equally with others in the exercise of political power." See Rawls (1999b), p. 146.

9 Martin (1985), p. 55.

10 For further considerations against the feasibility of equalizing the worth of the basic liberties see Krouse and McPherson (1988), p. 85.

11 See Daniels (1989b), pp. 253–81.

12 Daniels (1989b), p. 255.

13 Because the principle of equal liberty has priority over the second principle, Daniels thinks that if institutional design did not suffice to protect equal opportunities for political influence, the new version of the theory would support limiting economic inequalities to prevent them from generating a highly unequal distribution of political power. See Daniels (1989a), p. xxiv. Rawls' brief endorsement of the economic system of a property-owning democracy seems to support the conclusion that the equalization of political power among citizens requires a dispersion of property: that is, that it requires a reduction of economic inequality.

14 This point is examined by Brighouse (1997).

15 See Berlin (2002), pp. 166–217.

16 One problem with appealing to autonomy in a political theory of justice is that there are too many accounts of what counts as being or acting autonomously. Some of these accounts are quite demanding and would label many people as lacking autonomy. Depending on the account of autonomy, domination may either impede its development, or seriously restrict its exercise, or block its exercise completely.

17 This is not a direct quotation, but seems to be the clearest statement of his present view. See Pettit (1999), pp. 52–58; Pettit (2005), pp. 92–94. The following three paragraphs are based largely on Costa (2009b), pp. 404–406.

18 In my view, Pettit's notion of arbitrary interference by private parties is clearer than his notion of arbitrary interference by the state. One reason for this is that we have a fairly clear pre-theoretical sense of what the central interests of individuals are. The notion of arbitrary interference by the state is more problematic because of difficulties in giving a precise sense to what the common interests of citizens are, particularly when it comes to deciding policies about which there is

reasonable disagreement. For discussions on the problem of determining what counts as state domination see McMahon (2005); Pettit (2006); Costa (2007).

19 But see Rawls (2001), pp. 130–32.

20 For additional arguments that Rawls owes a debt to the Republican tradition, see De Francisco (2006); Laden (2006); Larmore (2008).

21 For a detailed examination of the democratic elements of Rawls' theory, see Cohen (2003).

22 The requirement that laws dealing with constitutional essentials and matters of basic justice be justified in terms of public reasons is another element in the theory that provides some assurance against state domination of citizens. But it is worth noting that this requirement only applies to constitutional essentials and matters of basic justice. Moreover, the requirement that citizens use public reasons in political debates is a moral duty of citizens, according to Rawls. As such, it cannot be enforced. And for this reason it cannot alter structural relationships of domination. See Rawls (1999b), pp. 136.

23 See Rawls (1996), pp. 324–63.

24 Rawls (2001), p. 131.

25 I provide a more detailed discussion of the problem of specifying the common interests of citizens, as dealt with in Pettit's later works in Costa (2007).

26 Pettit (2008), pp. 201–23.

27 Rawls (1999a), p. 63.

28 It is a controversial question, what kinds of policies of affirmative action the fair equality of opportunity principle would support in non-ideal contexts. See Taylor (2009).

29 Mason (2006), pp. 72–73.

30 Rawls (2001), pp. 135–48. Also see Freeman (2007), pp. 133–36, 219–35; Krouse and McPherson (1988).

31 Krouse and McPherson (1988), pp. 91–92.

32 Rawls (2001), p. 164.

33 Rawls (2001), p. 167.

34 The exception is Laborde (2008). But Laborde is not trying to defend an education for non-domination that is compatible with Rawls' political approach to the justification of policy.

35 For a small sample see Brighouse (1998); Burtt (2003); Callan (1997); Levinson (1999).

36 See Rawls (2001), pp. 142–45.

37 Rawls' requirement that a just society provide equal support for the self-respect of its citizens can be used as the basis for justifying an education that targets attitudes of servility, which is the unfortunate result of some instances of interpersonal domination. There is an abundant literature on what Rawls means by self-respect, on whether the social bases of self-respect qualify as primary goods, and, if so, how they can be distributed equally. I am not trying to settle these issues here. My point is only that if one accepts Rawls' claims about the importance of securing citizens' self-respect, this provides some grounds for an education that targets attitudes of servility.

38 See Hill (1973). For an alternative account of servility see Callan (1997), pp. 152–59.

39 Hill (1973), p. 90.

40 Hampton (1997), p. 23.

Chapter 7

1 For examples of civic virtues that are compatible with Rawls' political approach, see Costa (2004).

2 Callan (2002), p. 468. Callan acknowledges that there are differences between identification with one's nation and identification with one's state. See Callan (2004), p. 78.

3 Miller (1995b), pp. 153–66.

4 Taylor (1989), pp. 159–82.

5 The use of the word 'patriotism' certainly covers a range of different phenomena, including feelings of attachment to and identification with one's native land, its language, scenery, culture, and history, as well as feelings of allegiance to one's political community. For other definitions of patriotism, see Keller (2005); Kleingeld (2000). I will examine some issues raised by nationalism in the context of multination states in chapter 8.

6 For an extension and application of Rawls' theory of justice to a discussion of the justice of restrictions on the freedom to immigrate see Carens (1987). Rawls' own work on international justice suggests he would neither agree with Carens' method of extension of justice as fairness, nor endorse Carens' conclusions. See Rawls (1999b), p. 9.

7 Rawls (1996), pp. 30–35.

8 Rawls claims that we have a natural duty to support and comply with just institutions. This implies that citizens have a duty to support and comply with the institutions of their own state, assuming it is reasonably just. But obviously this is a far cry from the idea that good citizens should be patriotic. See Rawls (1999a), §19.

9 It is worth mentioning that Rawls' ideal model of a closed society into which citizens are born and in which they live out their entire lives makes it impossible to raise issues relating to immigration and naturalization. In his later ideal theory of international justice he admits the possibility of immigration but claims it would not be significant if most countries in the world were just or decent. See Rawls (1999b), p. 9.

10 See Miller (1995a), p. 93; Tamir (1993), pp. 117–39.

11 Tamir (1993), chapter 6.

12 Tamir (1993), p. 118.

13 I owe this point to Eamonn Callan.

14 See Rawls (1999b).

15 One might hold that Rawls' peoples include multinational states. However, see Rawls (1999b), p. 23, where Rawls makes reference to the notion of shared nationality as one of the defining features of peoples. For a more extensive argument that Rawls' peoples are nations, see Buchanan (2000), pp. 698–99.

16 See Carens (2000), pp. 161–76.

17 Rawls (1999a), p. 413.

18 Callan (1997), p. 93.

19 For a diametrically opposed view of Rawls' account of citizenship and its psychological preconditions, see Hill (1993). In my view, it is interesting that both Callan's and Hill's interpretation of Rawls' account of the development of a sense of justice in citizens are plausible. But Hill appeals to Rawls to argue *against* the need for patriotism. My conclusion is that Rawls' text does not have a clear commitment one way or the other.

20 See Callan (2006), pp. 525–46.

21 Moore (1999), pp. 475–76.

22 Brighouse (2003), p. 163.

23 Callan (2002), pp. 465–67.

24 McDonough (2003). Much will depend on the kind of patriotism that the state and schools are encouraging. But even if the kind of patriotism encouraged is of a benign and humane form, distrust resulting from past injustices may make minority groups find patriotic policies threatening.

25 Miller (2007), pp. 7–21.

26 Callan (2004), p. 81.

27 For defenses of a patriotic history see Galston (1991), pp. 241–56; Nash (1996); Fullinwider (1996b); Callan (1997), pp. 100–131.

28 This has been the predominant trend in Argentina. See Romero et al. (2004). For evidence of this trend in the United States see Loewen (1995) and Nash (1996). On the teaching of patriotism in the United Kingdom, see Archard (1999), pp. 157–58.

29 This discussion of Galston's views on civic education relies heavily on Costa (2006), pp. 280–85.

30 Galston (1991), p. 242.

31 Galston (1991), p. 243–44.

32 The expression is from Fullinwider (1996b), though he is less willing to distort the truth in service of loyalty.

33 Callan (1997), pp. 105–8.

34 One exception here is that beliefs in patriotic myths may prompt some to volunteer to fight for their country in defense of causes that they would not endorse if they had a more accurate perception of the situation.

35 I owe this example to María Julia Bertomeu.

36 Romero et al. (2004), pp. 69–73.

37 See Nash (1996), pp. 183–202; Callan (2002), pp. 465–77.

38 For a nice defense of the requirement of teaching with integrity, without distorting academic subjects for political purposes, see Strike (2004).

39 For more detailed recommendations and similar conclusions on the teaching of history see Brighouse (2003), pp. 168–74.

40 These distinctions are inspired by Andrew Mason's discussion of the sense of belonging. My own positive proposal differs from Mason's in that he thinks that what really matters is identification with (b), and not (a). See Mason (2000), pp. 115–47.

41 Mason (2000), p. 137.

Chapter 8

1 Rawls (1999f), p. 395.

2 Melissa Williams holds that there are no significant differences between Rawls and liberal patriots/liberal nationalists, since both rely on an overly restrictive account of citizen identity: they both expect good citizens to have a certain set of identifications and commitments. She thinks it would be less restrictive to focus on the cultivation of certain political virtues that would allow people with shared activities to work together in fair ways. But in fact the virtues she describes are political virtues that are very similar to those recommended by Rawls. And it seems unlikely to me that people could acquire these virtues without normative commitments of the kind that are summarized at least in the first principle of justice. See Williams (2003).

3 Liberal patriots/liberal nationalists who criticize Rawls generally have in mind actual societies, which are certainly more complex than the simplified model used by Rawls. They claim that, outside a Rawlsian well-ordered society, patriotism is even more necessary to generate trust, solidarity, and a willingness to make sacrifices for one's country and compatriots, among other desirable dispositions. See Callan (2002).

4 See Rawls (1999b), p. 177.

5 See Rawls (1999b), especially his remarks on immigration (p. 9) and on national identity (p. 23).

6 Rawls (1999a), p. 8.

7 This is not the exact formulation of the difference principle. I state it in this way because Rawls admits that there can be a range of acceptable principles of redistribution in actual societies. Moreover, it is easier to determine that the difference principle is not satisfied in a society than if it is satisfied. It is easier to say that existing social arrangements do not maximize the life prospects of the least advantaged than that the existing arrangements are actually optimal in light of this goal.

8 Rawls's discussion of perfectionism raises the question of whether the state is allowed to support science, arts, and cultural events. But this is not the sense of culture that is relevant to our present discussion. See Rawls (1999a), pp. 285–92.

9 Waldron (1996), p. 96.

10 The multicultural literature sometimes includes gays and lesbians, the disabled, and women as if they share a 'culture.' But it seems to me that this approach stretches the meaning of 'culture' too much. In contrast, some African American communities in the United States might be considered to be a cultural community in the sense I am endorsing. This would be the case for those who share distinctive cultural practices, particularly patterns of language, that work as barriers to their integration in the wider society. But racial prejudice and the legacy of segregation also prevent their integration, so it is unclear to me whether a focus on cultural differences would be helpful.

11 Rawls (1996), p. 222.

12 For a careful examination of such policies in the context of Canada and the United States see Kymlicka (1995).

13 See Kymlicka (2001), pp. 17–48.

14 For similar interpretations of Rawls on this issue see Kymlicka (1995), p. 128; Patten (2000), p. 195; and Levy (2007), p. 192.

15 See Kymlicka (1989a), pp. 162–81; Kymlicka (1995), pp. 75–130.

16 Kymlicka (1995), p. 76. Kymlicka uses the technical term "societal culture" to refer to a culture that is embodied in central social institutions, and he claims that people need access to a secure societal culture that is their own. I avoid this terminology because it makes it less clear what is at stake in the debate about the kinds of policies that should be adopted in multicultural societies. For a criticism of this technical notion of a societal culture see Carens (2000), pp. 54–73.

17 Many authors have criticized the sharp distinction Kymlicka's argument implies, between what national minorities are entitled to as a matter of justice, and what immigrant are entitled to. But when it comes to proposing actual policies, Kymlicka favors accommodating many demands of both kinds of groups.

18 I am not trying to settle the question of the justice of borders. My present concern is to stress that the policies that national minorities are "entitled" to pursue vary with the size, territorial concentration, and other aspects of the situation of these groups.

19 I am certainly simplifying the policies adopted in Quebec. For a detailed discussion see Carens (2000), pp. 107–39; Kymlicka (1998), part 2.

20 Kymlicka (1995), p. 86.

21 For an interesting overview of the multicultural theory and its methodological commitments, which emphasizes Kymlicka's contributions to the field, see Levy (2007).

22 Carens (2000), pp. 59–60.

23 See Waldron (1992). For a discussion of Waldron's cultural cosmopolitanism and its implications for civic education see McDonough (1997) and Costa (2005).

24 In fact, Waldron also suggests that Rawls' picture of individuals adopting and pursuing a conception of the good life is too rigid: people seem just to choose to pursue different activities from time to time without any overall, structured, plan of life. See Waldron (1992), p. 753.

25 Waldron (1992), p. 754.

26 For an extended argument, see Waldron (2003).

27 Waldron (1992), p. 763.

28 This happens when he argues for the status of cultural belonging as a basic good that is essential to the exercise of personal freedom in Kymlicka (1989a) and Kymlicka (1995). But in his later papers his position is more nuanced. See Kymlicka (1998); Kymlicka (2003).

29 See Waldron (2003), p. 47, footnote 22.

30 Kymlicka distinguishes between citizens' support for multicultural policies at the state level and citizens' willingness to interact with members of society who have a different cultural background from their own. This distinction is important because we can think of societies in which the state accommodates cultural differences while members of cultural communities prefer to live in relative isolation from each other, as if they were parallel societies within the borders of one state. See Kymlicka (2003).

31 Carens (2005); Callan (unpublished).

32 National minorities sometimes aspire to a certain degree of self-government and make a number of demands on the rest of society. It is not possible to assess the reasonability of these kinds of demands in the abstract, independently of the particular situation and history of the society and its groups. But the accommodation of such demands should be consistent with the first principle of justice that guarantees the basic rights and liberties of individuals, regardless of group membership.

33 For an interesting discussion of theories about 'multiculturalism' see Yack (2002). About the wide appeal of 'multiculturalism' in educational debates, with a focus on the United States, see Glazer (1997); Reich (2002).

34 See Kymlicka (1998); Callan (unpublished).

35 Here I follow but modify some of the recommendations in Kymlicka (1998), pp. 200–208.

36 See Spinner-Halev (2007).

37 Kymlicka has argued that these kinds of multicultural policies do have integrative effects, at least in the case of immigrants. In order to measure such effects, social scientists study immigrants in countries with multicultural policies, and compare their behavior with that of the native population. They measure, for example, whether immigrants and their children are geographically mixed, whether they marry and make friends outside their cultural group, and their levels of educational, professional, and economic achievement. See Kymlicka (1998), pp. 15–24; Citrin et al. (2007). Things are more complicated when one turns to the situation of national minorities in societies with a recent history of conflicts between national groups and pervasive distrust between them. In these cases, which cannot be assessed in the abstract, social policies that aim at promoting integration may not lead to more just social arrangements. Relatively separated institutions may be the second best feasible policy, at least until many years of peaceful coexistence have passed. In such suboptimal circumstances, forms of separate schooling may be preferable. See Spinner-Halev (2003).

Bibliography

Ackerman, Bruce (1980), *Social Justice in the Liberal State* (New Haven: Yale University Press).

Anderson, Elizabeth (2002), "Integration, Affirmative Action, and Strict Scrutiny," *New York University Law Review* 77, 5: 1195–1271.

——(2004), "Rethinking Equality of Opportunity: Comment on Adam Swift's How Not to be a Hypocrite," *Theory and Research in Education* 2, 2: 99–110.

——(2007), "Fair Opportunity in Education: A Democratic Equality Perspective," *Ethics* 117, 4: 595–622.

Archard, David (1999), "Should We Teach Patriotism?" *Studies in Philosophy and Education* 18, 3: 157–73.

Archard, David and Colin Macleod eds. (2002), *The Moral and Political Status of Children* (Oxford: Oxford University Press).

Arneson, Richard and Ian Shapiro (1996), "Democratic Autonomy and Religious Freedom: A Critique of Wisconsin v. Yoder," in Shapiro and Hardin (1996): 365–411.

Baehr, Amy (1996), "Toward a New Feminist Liberalism: Okin, Rawls, and Habermas," *Hypatia* 11, 1: 49–66.

Baron, Marcia (1985), "Servility, Critical Deference and the Deferential Wife," *Philosophical Studies* 48, 3: 393–400.

Barry, Brian (1995), "John Rawls and the Search for Stability," *Ethics* 105, 4: 874–915.

——(2001), *Culture and Equality: An Egalitarian Critique of Multiculturalism* (Cambridge: Harvard University Press).

Barry, Christian (2003), "Education and Standards of Living," in Curren (2003): 456–70.

Benhabib, Seyla (2002), *The Claims of Culture: Equality and Diversity in the Global Era* (Princeton: Princeton University Press).

——(2004), *The Rights of Others: Aliens, Residents and Citizens* (Cambridge: Cambridge University Press).

Berlin, Isaiah (2002), "Two Concepts of Liberty," in Isaiah Berlin, *Liberty*, ed. Henry Hardy (Oxford: Oxford University Press), pp. 166–217.

Bertomeu, María Julia, Antoni Doménech, and Andrés De Francisco eds. (2005), *Republicanismo y Democracia* (Madrid: Miño y Dávila).

Bojer, Hilde (2000), "Children and Theories of Distributional Justice," *Feminist Economics* 6, 2: 23–29.

——(2002), "Women and the Rawlsian Social Contract," *Social Justice Research* 15, 4: 393–407.

Brake, Elizabeth (2004), "Rawls and Feminism: What Should Feminists Make of Liberal Neutrality?" *Journal of Moral Philosophy* 1, 3: 295–312.

Brennan, Samantha and Robert Noggle (2000), "Rawls's Neglected Childhood: Reflections on the Original Position, Stability, and the Child's Sense of Justice," in Davion and Wolf (2000): 46–72.

——eds. (2007), *Taking Responsibility for Children* (Waterloo: Wilfrid Laurier University Press).

Brighouse, Harry (1997), "Political Equality in Justice as Fairness," *Philosophical Studies* 86, 2: 155–84.

——(1998), "Civic Education and Liberal Legitimacy," *Ethics* 108, 4: 719–45.

——(2000), *School Choice and Social Justice* (Oxford: Oxford University Press).

——(2003), "Should We Teach Patriotic History?" in McDonough and Feinberg (2003): 157–75.

Brighouse, Harry and Adam Swift (2008), "Putting Educational Equality in Its Place," *Education Finance and Policy* 3, 4: 444–66.

——(2009a), "Educational Equality versus Educational Adequacy: A Critique of Anderson and Satz," *Journal of Applied Philosophy* 26, 2: 117–28.

——(2009b), "Legitimate Parental Partiality," *Philosophy and Public Affairs* 37, 1: 43–80.

Buchanan, Allen (2000), "Rawls's Law of Peoples: Rules for a Vanished Westphalian World," *Ethics* 110, 4: 697–721.

Bull, Barry, Royal Fruehling, and Virgie Chattergy (1992), *The Ethics of Multicultural and Bilingual Education* (New York: Teachers College Press).

Burtt, Shelly (1996), "In Defense of Yoder: Parental Authority and the Public Schools," in Shapiro and Hardin (1996): 412–37.

——(2002), "What Children Really Need: Towards a Critical Theory of Family Structure," in Archard and Macleod (2002): 231–52.

——(2003), "Comprehensive Educations and the Liberal Understanding of Autonomy," in McDonough and Feinberg (2003): 179–207.

Callan, Eamonn (1997), *Creating Citizens: Political Education and Liberal Democracy* (Oxford: Oxford University Press).

——(2002), "Democratic Patriotism and Multicultural Education," *Studies in Philosophy and Education* 21, 6: 465–77.

——(2004), "Citizenship and Education," *Annual Review of Political Science* 7: 71–90.

——(2005), "The Ethics of Assimilation," *Ethics* 115, 3: 471–500.

——(2006), "Love, Idolatry, and Patriotism," *Social Theory and Practice* 32, 4: 525–46.

——"Integrating Immigrants," unpublished manuscript.

Carens, Joseph (1987), "Aliens and Citizens: The Case for Open Borders," *Review of Politics* 49, 2: 251–73.

——(2000), *Culture, Citizenship, and Community: A Contextual Exploration of Justice as Evenhandedness* (Oxford: Oxford University Press).

——(2005), "The Integration of Immigrants," *Journal of Moral Philosophy* 2, 1: 29–46.

Chambers, Simone and Jeffrey Kopstein (2001), "Bad Civil Society," *Political Theory* 29, 6: 837–65.

Citrin, Jack, Amy Lerman, Michael Murakami, and Kathryn Pearson (2007), "Testing Huntington: Is Hispanic Immigration a Threat to American Identity?" *Perspectives on Politics* 5, 1: 31–48.

Clayton, Matthew (2006), *Justice and Legitimacy in Upbringing* (Oxford: Oxford University Press).

Cohen, Gerald (2000), *If You're an Egalitarian, How Come You're So Rich?* (Cambridge: Harvard University Press).

Cohen, Joshua (1992), "Okin on Justice, Gender, and Family," *Canadian Journal of Philosophy* 22, 2: 263–86.

——(2003), "For a Democratic Society," in Freeman (2003): 86–138.

Costa, M. Victoria (2004), "Political Liberalism and the Complexity of Civic Virtue," *Southern Journal of Philosophy* 42, 2: 149–70.

——(2005), "Cultural Cosmopolitanism and Civic Education," *Philosophy of Education*: 250–58.

——(2006), "Galston on Liberal Virtues and the Aims of Civic Education," *Theory and Research in Education* 4, 3: 275–89.

——(2007), "Freedom as Non-Domination, Normativity and Indeterminacy," *Journal of Value Inquiry* 41, 2/4: 291–307.

——(2009a), "Citizenship and the State," *Philosophy Compass* 4, 6: 987–97.

——(2009b), "Neo-Republicanism, Freedom as Non-Domination and Citizen Virtue," *Politics, Philosophy and Economics* 8, 4: 401–19.

Curren, Randall (1994), "Justice and the Threshold of Educational Equality," *Philosophy of Education*: 239–48.

——ed. (2003), *A Companion to the Philosophy of Education* (Malden: Blackwell).

Daniels, Norman (1989a), *Reading Rawls: Critical Studies on Rawls' 'A Theory of Justice'* (Stanford: Stanford University Press).

——(1989b), "Equal Liberty and Unequal Worth of Liberty," in Daniels (1989a): 253–81.

——(1996), *Justice and Justification: Reflective Equilibrium in Theory and Practice* (Cambridge: Cambridge University Press).

——(2003), "Democratic Equality: Rawls' Complex Egalitarianism," in Freeman (2003): 241–76.

Davion, Victoria and Clark Wolf eds. (2000), *The Idea of a Political Liberalism: Essays on Rawls* (Lanham: Rowman & Littlefield).

De Francisco, Andrés (2006), "A Republican Interpretation of the Late Rawls," *The Journal of Political Philosophy* 14, 3: 270–88.

De Marneffe, Peter (2002), "Liberalism, Neutrality and Education," in Macedo and Tamir (2002): 221–43.

English, Jane (1977), "Justice between Generations," *Philosophical Studies* 31, 2: 91–104.

Feinberg, Walter (1998), *Common Schools/Uncommon Identities: National Unity and Cultural Difference* (New Haven: Yale University Press).

——(2003), "Religious Education in Liberal Democratic Societies: The Question of Accountability and Autonomy," in McDonough and Feinberg (2003): 385–413.

Fishkin, James (1983), *Justice, Equal Opportunity, and the Family* (New Haven: Yale University Press).

Freeman, Samuel ed. (1999), *Collected Papers* (Cambridge: Harvard University Press).

——ed. (2003), *The Cambridge Companion to Rawls* (Cambridge: Cambridge University Press).

——(2007), *Rawls* (London: Routledge).

Friedman, Marilyn (1985), "Moral Integrity and the Deferential Wife," *Philosophical Studies* 47, 1: 141–50.

Fullinwider, Robert ed. (1996a), *Public Education in a Multicultural Society: Policy, Theory, Critique* (Cambridge: Cambridge University Press).

——(1996b), "Patriotic History," in Fullinwider (1996a): 203–27.

——(2003), "Multicultural Education," in Curren (2003): 487–500.

Galeotti, Anna Elisabetta (1996), "Political Toleration or Politics of Recognition: The Headscarves Affair Revisited," *Political Theory* 24, 2: 315–20.

Galston, William (1991), *Liberal Purposes: Goods, Virtues, and Diversity in the Liberal State* (Cambridge: Cambridge University Press).

——(1995), "Two Concepts of Liberalism," *Ethics* 105, 3: 516–34.

——(2002), *Liberal Pluralism: The Implications of Value Pluralism for Political Theory and Practice* (Cambridge: Cambridge University Press).

Garreta, Mariano (2001), "La Concepción Liberal de 'Persona Razonable': Una Propuesta de Justificación," *Análisis Filosófico* 21, 2: 217–64.

Gilligan, Carol (1982), *In a Different Voice: Psychological Theory and Women's Development* (Cambridge: Harvard University Press).

Glazer, Nathan (1997), *We Are All Multiculturalists Now* (Cambridge: Harvard University Press).

Gutmann, Amy ed. (1988), *Democracy and the Welfare State* (Princeton: Princeton University Press).

——(1993), "The Challenge of Multiculturalism in Political Ethics," *Philosophy and Public Affairs* 22, 3: 171–206.

——(1995), "Civic Education and Social Diversity," *Ethics* 105, 3: 557–79.

Halstead, Mark (1999), "Moral Education in Family Life: the Effects of Diversity," *Journal of Moral Education* 28, 3: 265–81.

——(2003), "Schooling and Cultural Maintenance for Religious Minorities in the Liberal State," in McDonough and Feinberg (2003): 273–95.

Hampton, Jean (1997), "The Wisdom of the Egoist: The Moral and Political Implications of Valuing the Self," *Social Philosophy and Policy* 14, 1: 21–51.

Hart, H.L.A. (1989), "Rawls on Liberty and its Priority," in Daniels (1989a): 230–52.

Hill, Greg (1993), "Citizenship and Ontology in the Liberal State," *Review of Politics* 55, 1: 67–84.

Hill, Thomas (1973), "Servility and Self-Respect," *The Monist* 57, 1: 87–104.

Kaufman, Alexander (2006), "Rawls's Practical Conception of Justice: Opinion, Tradition and Objectivity in Political Liberalism," *Journal of Moral Philosophy* 3, 1: 23–43.

Kearns, Deborah (1983), "A Theory of Justice – and Love; Rawls on the Family," *Politics* 18, 2: 36–42.

Keller, Simon (2005), "Patriotism as Bad Faith," *Ethics* 115, 3: 563–92.

Kleingeld, Pauline (2000), "Kantian Patriotism," *Philosophy and Public Affairs* 29, 4: 313–41.

Kohlberg, Lawrence (1984), *Essays on Moral Development* (San Francisco: Harper and Row).

Koski, William and Rob Reich (2006), "When 'Adequate' Isn't: The Retreat from Equity in Educational Law and Policy and Why It Matters," *Emory Law Journal* 56, 3: 545–617.

Kramer, Matthew, Claire Grant, Ben Colburn and Antony Hatzistavrou eds. (2008), *The Legacy of H. L. A. Hart: Legal, Political, and Moral Philosophy* (New York: Oxford University Press).

Krasnoff, Larry (1998), "Consensus, Stability, and Normativity in Rawls' Political Liberalism," *Journal of Philosophy* 95, 6: 269–92.

Krouse, Richard and Michael McPherson (1988), "Capitalism, 'Property-Owning Democracy' and the Welfare State," in Gutmann (1988): 79–105.

Kymlicka, Will (1989a), *Liberalism, Community and Culture* (Oxford: Clarendon Press).

——(1989b), "Liberal Individualism and Liberal Neutrality," *Ethics* 99, 4: 883–905.

——(1991), "Rethinking the Family," *Philosophy and Public Affairs* 20, 1: 77–97.

——(1995), *Multicultural Citizenship: A Liberal Theory of Minority Rights* (Oxford: Clarendon Press).

——(1998), *Finding Our Way: Rethinking Ethnocultural Relations in Canada* (Toronto: Oxford University Press).

——(2001), *Politics in the Vernacular: Nationalism, Multiculturalism, and Citizenship* (Oxford: Oxford University Press).

——(2003), "Multicultural States and Intercultural Citizens," *Theory and Research in Education* 1, 2: 147–69.

Kymlicka, Will and Wayne Norman (1994), "Return of the Citizen: A Survey of Recent Work on Citizenship Theory," *Ethics* 104, 2: 352–81.

Laborde, Cécile (2008), *Critical Republicanism: The Hijab Controversy and Political Philosophy* (Oxford: Oxford University Press).

Laden, Anthony (2006), "Republican Moments in Political Liberalism," *Revue Internationale de Philosophie* 237, 3: 341–67.

Laden, Anthony and David Owen eds. (2007), *Multiculturalism and Political Theory* (Cambridge: Cambridge University Press).

Larmore, Charles (1987), *Patterns of Moral Complexity* (Cambridge: Cambridge University Press).

——(2008), *The Autonomy of Morality* (Cambridge: Cambridge University Press).

Levinson, Meira (1999), *The Demands of Liberal Education* (Oxford: Oxford University Press).

Levy, Jacob (2007), "Contextualism, Constitutionalism, and Modus Vivendi Approaches," in Laden and Owen (2007): 173–97.

Lloyd, S.A. (1995), "Situating the Feminist Criticism of John Rawls' *Political Liberalism*," *Loyola LA Law Review* 28: 1319–44.

Loewen, J. W. (1995), *Lies my Teacher Told Me: Everything your American History Textbook got Wrong* (New York: Touchstone).

Lomasky, Loren (1987), *Persons, Rights, and the Moral Community* (New York: Oxford University Press).

MacCallum, Gerald (1967), "Negative and Positive Freedom," *Philosophical Review* 76, 3: 312–34.

Macedo, Stephen (1995), "Liberal Civic Education and Religious Fundamentalism: The Case of God v. John Rawls?" *Ethics* 105, 3: 468–96.

——(2000), *Diversity and Distrust: Civic Education in a Multicultural Democracy* (Cambridge: Harvard University Press).

Macedo, Stephen and Yael Tamir eds. (2002), *Nomos 43: Moral and Political Education* (New York: New York University Press).

Macedo, Stephen and Melissa Williams (2005), *Nomos 46: Political Exclusion and Domination* (New York: New York University Press).

Macedo, Stephen and Iris Marion Young eds. (2003), *Nomos 44: Child, Family and State* (New York: New York University Press).

MacIntyre, Alasdair (1990), "The Privatization of Good," *Review of Politics* 52, 3: 344–61.

Macleod, Colin (2002), "Liberal Equality and the Affective Family," in Archard and Macleod (2002): 212–30.

MacMullen, Ian (2007), *Faith in Schools? Autonomy, Citizenship, and Religious Education in the Liberal State* (Princeton: Princeton University Press).

Mandle, Jon (2000), *What's Left of Liberalism? An Interpretation and Defense of Justice as Fairness* (Lanham: Lexington Books).

Martin, Rex (1985), *Rawls and Rights* (Lawrence: University Press of Kansas).

Mason, Andrew (2000), *Community, Solidarity and Belonging: Levels of Community and Their Normative Significance* (Cambridge: Cambridge University Press).

——(2006), *Levelling the Playing Field: The Idea of Equal Opportunity and Its Place in Egalitarian Thought* (Oxford: Oxford University Press).

McCabe, David (1998), "Private Lives and Public Virtues: the Idea of a Liberal Community," *Canadian Journal of Philosophy* 28, 4: 557–86.

McDonough, Kevin (1997), "Cultural Recognition, Cosmopolitanism and Multicultural Education," *Philosophy of Education*: 127–35.

——(1998), "Can the Liberal State Support Cultural Identity Schools?" *American Journal of Education* 106, 4: 463–99.

——(2003), "Multinational Civic Education," in McDonough and Feinberg (2003), pp. 351–84.

McDonough, Kevin and Walter Feinberg eds. (2003), *Education and Citizenship in Liberal Democratic Societies: Teaching for Cosmopolitan Values and Collective Identities* (Oxford: Oxford University Press).

Mckinnon Catriona and Iain Hampsher-Monk eds. (2000), *Demands of Citizenship* (London: Continuum).

McLaughlin, Terence (1992), "Citizenship, Diversity and Education: a Philosophical Perspective", *Journal of Moral Education* 21, 3: 235–50.

——(1995), "Liberalism, Education and the Common School", *Journal of Philosophy of Education* 29, 2: 239–55.

McMahon, Christopher (2005), "The Indeterminacy of Republican Policy," *Philosophy and Public Affairs* 33,1: 67–93.

Miller, David (1995a), *On Nationality* (Oxford: Oxford University Press).

——(1995b), "Reflections on British National Identity," *New Community* 21, 2: 153–66.

Miller, Richard (2007), "Unlearning American Patriotism," *Theory and Research in Education* 5, 1: 7–21.

Mills, Charles (2005), "'Ideal theory' as Ideology," *Hypatia* 20, 3: 165–84.

Moore, Margaret (1999), "Nationalist Arguments, Ambivalent Conclusions," *The Monist* 82, 3: 469–90.

——(2001), *The Ethics of Nationalism* (Oxford: Oxford University Press).

Mulhall, Steven (1998), "Political Liberalism and Civic Education," *Journal of Philosophy of Education* 32, 2: 161–76.

Munoz-Dardé, Véronique (1998), "Rawls, Justice in the Family and Justice of the Family," *Philosophical Quarterly* 48, 192: 335–52.

——(1999), "Is the Family to be Abolished then?" *Proceedings of the Aristotelian Society* 99: 37–56.

Murphy, Liam (1999), "Institutions and the Demands of Justice," *Philosophy and Public Affairs* 27, 4: 251–91.

Nash, Gary (1996), "Multiculturalism and History: Historical Perspectives and Present Prospects," in Fullinwider (1996a): 183–202.

Nickel, James (1993/1994), "Rethinking Rawls' Theory of Liberty and Rights," *Chicago-Kent Law Review* 69, 3: 763–85.

Nino, Carlos (1992), *Un País al Margen de la Ley: Estudio de la Anomia como Componente del Subdesarrollo Argentino* (Buenos Aires: Emecé).

Norman, Wayne (1998), "'Inevitable and Unacceptable?' Methodological Rawlsianism in Anglo-American Political Philosophy," *Political Studies* 46, 2: 276–94.

Nussbaum, Martha (2003), "Rawls and Feminism," in Freeman (2003): 488–520.

Okin, Susan M. (1989), *Justice, Gender and the Family* (New York: Basic Books).

——(1994), "*Political Liberalism*, Justice and Gender," *Ethics* 105, 1: 23–43.

——(1996), "Sexual Orientation and Gender: Dichotomizing Differences," *Hypatia* 11, 1: 30–48.

——(1999), *Is Multiculturalism Bad for Women?* Joshua Cohen, Matthew Howard, and Martha Nussbaum eds. (Princeton: Princeton University Press).

——(2004), "Justice and Gender: An Unfinished Debate," *Fordham Law Review* 72, 5: 1537–67.

Okin, Susan M. and Rob Reich (1999), "Families and Schools as Compensating Agents in Moral Development for a Multicultural Society," *Journal of Moral Education* 28, 3: 283–98.

Parekh, Bhikhu (2000), *Rethinking Multiculturalism: Cultural Diversity and Political Theory* (Cambridge: Harvard University Press).

Parry, Geraint (1999), "Constructive and Reconstructive Political Education," *Oxford Review of Education* 25, 1/2: 21–38.

Patten, Alan (2000), "Equality of Recognition and the Liberal Theory of Citizenship," in Mckinnon and Hampsher-Monk (2000): 193–211.

Pettit, Philip (1999), *Republicanism: A Theory of Freedom and Government* (Oxford: Oxford University Press).

——(2005), "The Domination Complaint," in Williams and Macedo (2005): 87–117.

——(2006), "The Determinacy of Republican Policy: A Reply to McMahon," *Philosophy and Public Affairs* 34, 3: 275–83.

——(2008), "The Basic Liberties," in Kramer et al. (2008): 201–23.

Piaget, Jean (1932), *The Moral Judgment of the Child* (New York: Harcourt Brace).

Pogge, Thomas (1989), *Realizing Rawls* (Ithaca: Cornell University Press).

——(2007), *John Rawls: His Life and Theory of Justice* (Oxford: Oxford University Press).

Rawls, John (1996), *Political Liberalism*, revised edn. (New York: Columbia University Press).

——(1999a), *A Theory of Justice*, revised edn. (Cambridge: Harvard University Press).

——(1999b), *The Law of Peoples: with "The Idea of Public Reason Revisited"* (Cambridge: Harvard University Press).

——(1999c), "Social Unity and Primary Goods," in Freeman (1999): 359–87.

——(1999d), "The Domain of the Political and Overlapping Consensus," in Freeman (1999): 473–96.

——(1999e), "Kantian Constructivism in Moral Theory," in Freeman (1999): 303–58.

——(1999f), "Justice as Fairness: Political not Metaphysical," in Freeman (1999): 388–414.

——(2001), *Justice as Fairness: A Restatement*, Erin Kelly ed. (Cambridge: Harvard University Press).

Reich, Rob (2002), *Bridging Liberalism and Multiculturalism in American Education* (Chicago: University of Chicago Press).

Richardson, Henry (2006), "Disabilities, Capabilities, and Rawlsian Social Contract Theory," *The Journal of Ethics* 10, 4: 419–62.

Romero, Luis Alberto, Luciano de Privitellio, Silvina Quintero, and Hilda Sábato (2004), *La Argentina en la Escuela: La Idea de Nación en los Textos Escolares* (Buenos Aires: Siglo XXI).

Rorty, Amelie ed. (1998), *Philosophers Discuss Education* (London: Routledge).

Rosenblum, Nancy ed. (1989), *Liberalism and the Moral Life* (Cambridge: Harvard University Press).

——(1994), "Democratic Character and Community: The Logic of Congruence?" *Journal of Political Philosophy* 2, 1: 67–97.

Sandel, Michael (1998), *Liberalism and the Limits of Justice*, second edn. (Cambridge: Cambridge University Press).

Sangiovanni, Andrea (2008), "Justice and the Priority of Politics to Morality," *Journal of Political Philosophy* 16, 2: 137–64.

Satz, Debra (2007), "Equality, Adequacy and Education for Citizenship," *Ethics* 117, 4: 623–48.

——(2008), "Equality, Adequacy, and Educational Policy," *Education Finance and Policy* 3, 4: 424–43.

Satz, Debra and Reich, Rob eds. (2009), *Toward a Humanist Justice: The Political Philosophy of Susan Moller Okin* (Oxford: Oxford University Press).

Schaller, Walter (1998), "Rawls, the Difference Principle, and Economic Inequality," *Pacific Philosophical Quarterly* 79, 4: 368–91.

Scheffler, Samuel (2007), "Immigration and the Significance of Culture," *Philosophy and Public Affairs* 35, 2: 93–125.

Shapiro, Ian and Russell Hardin (1996), *Nomos 38: Political Order* (New York: State University of New York Press).

Skinner, Quentin (1983), "Machiavelli on the Maintenance of Liberty," *Politics* 18, 2: 3–15.

Spinner-Halev, Jeff (2000), *Surviving Diversity: Religion and Democratic Citizenship* (Baltimore: Johns Hopkins University Press).

——(2003), "Education, Reconciliation and Nested Identities," *Theory and Research in Education* 1, 1: 51–72.

——(2007), "From Historical to Enduring Injustice," *Political Theory* 35, 5: 574–97.

Spitz, Jean-Fabien (1993), "The Concept of Liberty in 'A Theory of Justice' and Its Republican Version," *Ratio Juris* 7, 3: 331–47.

Strike, Kenneth (1982), *Educational Policy and the Just Society* (Urbana: University of Illinois Press).

——(1989), *Liberal Justice and the Marxist Critique of Education: A Study of Conflicting Research Programs* (New York: Routledge).

——(1993), "Ethical Discourse and Pluralism," in Strike and Ternasky (1993): 176–88.

——(1994), "On the Construction of Public Speech: Pluralism and Public Reason," *Educational Theory* 44, 1: 1–26.

——(2004), "Is Liberal Education Illiberal? Political Liberalism and Liberal Education," *Philosophy of Education*: 321–29.

Strike, Kenneth and Lance Ternasky eds. (1993), *Ethics for Professionals in Education* (New York: Teachers College Press)

Swift, Adam (1993), "Response to Spitz," *Ratio Juris* 7, 3: 348–52.

Tamir, Yael (1993), *Liberal Nationalism* (Princeton: Princeton University Press).

Taylor, Charles (1989), "Cross-Purposes: The Liberal-Communitarian Debate," in Rosenblum (1989): 159–82.

——(1992), *Multiculturalism and 'The Politics of Recognition'*, Amy Gutmann ed. (Princeton: Princeton University Press).

Taylor, Robert (2009), "Rawlsian Affirmative Action," *Ethics* 119, 3: 476–506.

Tomasi, John (2001), *Liberalism beyond Justice: Citizens, Society and the Boundaries of Political Theory* (Princeton: Princeton University Press).

Van Parijs, Philippe (2003), "Difference Principles," in Freeman (2003): 200–240.

Waldron, Jeremy (1992), "Minority Cultures and the Cosmopolitan Alternative," *University of Michigan Journal of Law Reform* 25, 3/4: 751–93.

——(1996), "Multiculturalism and Melange," in Fullinwider (1996a): 90–118.

——(2003), "Teaching Cosmopolitan Right," in McDonough and Feinberg (2003): 23–55.

Wall, Steven (2006), "Rawls and the Status of Political Liberty," *Pacific Philosophical Quarterly* 87, 2: 245–70.

Walzer, Michael (1983), *Spheres of Justice: A Defense of Pluralism and Equality* (New York: Basic Books).

Weinstock, Daniel (1999), "Neutralizing Perfection: Hurka on Liberal Neutrality," *Dialogue* 38, 1: 45–62.

Wenar, Leif (1995), "Political Liberalism: An Internal Critique," *Ethics* 106, 1: 32–62.

Williams, Melissa (2003), "Citizenship as Identity, Citizenship as Shared Fate, and the Functions of Multicultural Education," in McDonough and Feinberg (2003): 208–47.

Yack, Bernard (2002), "Multiculturalism and the Political Theorists," *European Journal of Political Theory* 1, 1: 107–19.

Young, Iris Marion (1994), "Making Single Motherhood Normal," *Dissent* 41, 1: 88–93.

——(2006), "Taking the Basic Structure Seriously," *Perspectives on Politics* 4, 1: 91–97.

Index

Ackerman, Bruce 136
altruism 89
Anderson, Elizabeth 134–35
Aristotle 1
assimilation 99, 113
autonomy: and domination 77–78, 127, 137; as an educational ideal 60, 63, 85–86, 126–27; Kantian 137; and perfectionism 69; political 69, 74, 86, 137

Barry, Brian 16
basic rights and liberties 15–16, 19–22, 36, 56, 73–74, 80–82, 86, 105, 131, 142; and the family 40–41; political liberties as 14, 16, 19, 21–22, 54, 73–76, 81, 87; *see also* freedom, liberty
basic structure of society 8–11, 18–19, 126–27; family as part of 38, 40–44, 125; global and domestic 130; health care system as part of 129–30; and individual behavior 25; school as part of 9, 125, 129
Berlin, Isaiah 77, 79
Brighouse, Harry 53–54, 99
burdens of judgment 27–29, 31, 33–35, 66–68, 98, 103–4, 132, 136

Callan, Eamonn 65, 67–68, 91, 95–101, 108, 129, 136, 139
care *see* work
Carens, Joseph 116, 139
citizens: as free and equal 1, 5, 11–12, 20, 27, 72–73, 77, 80–81, 92, 130; identity of 91–93, 95, 100, 140
civic knowledge *see* education in civics
civil society 58, 82; bad 58–59
coercion *see* threat

collective agents 74, 137
comprehensive doctrine 11–13, 17–18, 25–27, 31–34, 63, 66–69, 108–10, 132, 136; and culture 111–13; definition of reasonable 32–33
conception of the good: capacity for 12, 20, 27; and primary goods 14, 18
constitutional consensus 35–36
contestation of laws 79, 86–87, 90
cosmopolitanism 117
critical reflection 69, 86, 100–103
culture: accommodation of 115, 121, 123–24, 142; belonging to 114–17, 122, 142; benign neglect of 114; change of 118, 120–22; definition of 111–12; diversity of 7, 109–14; identity and 118–19; purity of 118–19; societal 141

Daniels, Norman 35, 75–76, 131, 137
De Marneffe, Peter 135
democracy 1, 3, 10–11, 36, 81; property-owning 24, 84, 137
Dewey, John 1
disability 42, 130–31, 141
discrimination 2, 22, 58–59, 70, 83, 105, 113, 123, 141
distribution of educational goods: adequacy in 134–35; and difference principle 55; and fair equality of opportunity principle 54; and first principle of justice 53–54; strict equality in 134; *see also* equality of opportunity in education
distribution of economic goods *see* principles of justice
diversity *see* ethnicity, pluralism, culture
domination 49, 78–79, 87; definition 78; by private parties 78, 80, 82, 87, 137;